**A RESEARCH STUDY COMMISSIONED BY THE
ONTARIO MINISTRY OF EDUCATION AND TRAINING**

Policies, Placement Practices, and Plans of Selected Ontario School Boards for Behavioural Exceptionalities and Developmental Challenges

Principal Investigators:
Janice A. Leroux
Barry H. Schneider

This research project was funded under contract by the Ministry of Education and Training, Ontario. It reflects the views of the authors and not necessarily those of the Ministry.

© QUEEN'S PRINTER FOR ONTARIO, 1994

Order Information:

MGS Publications Services
880 Bay Street, 5th Floor
Toronto, Ontario
M7A 1N8

(Toll Free in Ontario) 1-800-668-9938
(Out-of-province inquiries) (416) 326-5300

Order must be accompanied by a
cheque or money order payable
to the Treasurer of Ontario

371
.9042
09713
L618

AUG 1 2 1994

Canadian Cataloguing in Publication Data

Leroux, Janice A. (Janice Anne)
  Policies, placement practices, and plans of selected Ontario school boards for behavioural exceptionalities and developmental challenges

ISBN 0-7778-2755-7

1. Special education—Ontario. 2. Developmentally disabled—Ontario—Education.
I. Schneider, Barry H., 1949- . II. Ontario. Ministry of Education and Training.
III. Title.

LC3984.2O5L47 1994   371.9'042   C94-964035-2

TABLE OF CONTENTS

List of Figures and Tables vi

Acknowledgements viii

Sommaire ix

ORGANIZATION OF THE REPORT 1

Section 1

AN INTERNATIONAL SURVEY OF POLICIES AND PROCEDURES 2

Policies in Other Countries 3
Summary of Responses from Other Countries 13
Other Canadian Provinces 13
Summary of Responses from Other Canadian Provinces 18
Responses from Ontario School Boards 18
Comparison of Documents from Ontario and
  Those from Other Jurisdictions 22
References 23

Section 2

COMPARISON ACROSS JURISDICTIONS OF DEFINITIONS AND PREVALENCE RATES 24

Method 24
Results 25
Conclusions: Prevalence Rates 34
Canadian Definitions: Development Challenge 34
Canadian Definitions: Behaviour Disordered 35
Overseas Definitions: Trainable Retarded or
  Developmentally Challenged 37
Overseas Definitions: Behaviour Disordered 38
Conclusions: Definitional Issues 40
References 40

Section 3

EDUCATIONAL ENVIRONMENTS FOR THE BEHAVIOUR-DISORDERED PUPIL: A "BEST EVIDENCE" SYNTHESIS 41

    Challenges in Reviewing Literature 41
    Method 43
    Literature Search and Inclusion Rules 44
    Coding of Studies 44
    Results 44
    Conclusions 58
    References 58

Section 4

PROVINCE-WIDE PERSPECTIVE ON PLACEMENT AND PROGRAMMING FOR BEHAVIOUR-DISORDERED PUPILS 61

    Sampling Procedures 62
    Hypothetical Case Studies 63
    Semi-Structured Focus Group Interviews 65
    Telephone Interview Regarding Policy Development 69
    General Conclusions 70
    Concluding Summary 76
    References 76

Section 5

EDUCATIONAL ENVIRONMENTS FOR THE DEVELOPMENTALLY CHALLENGED PUPIL: A "BEST EVIDENCE" RESEARCH SYNTHESIS 77

    Challenges in Reviewing This Literature 77
    Method 78
    Literature Search and Inclusion Rules 79
    Coding of Studies 80
    Results 80
    Conclusions 82
    References 86

Section 6

PROVINCE-WIDE PERSPECTIVE ON PLACEMENT AND PROGRAMMING FOR DEVELOPMENTALLY CHALLENGED PUPILS 87

    Sampling Procedures 88
    Hypothetical Case Studies 89
    Semi-Structured Focus Group Interviews 91
    Telephone Interview Regarding Policy Development 95

General Conclusions 96
Reference 97

APPENDIX
INSTRUMENTS USED IN THE SEMI-STRUCTURED
FOCUS GROUP INTERVIEWS

    I. Questions Posed to Superintendents, Consultants and
       Special Services Personnel 98
   II. Questions Posed to Teachers 99
  III. Questions Posed to Parents 100

LIST OF FIGURES AND TABLES

Section 1

Figure 1.1	Focus of Placement Philosophy - Ontario Sample	20
Figure 1.2	Clusters of Placement Philosophies - Ontario Sample	20
Figure 1.3	Placement Policies - Ontario Sample	21
Figure 1.4	Range of Evaluation Procedures - Ontario Sample	22

Section 2

Table 2.1	Total Student Enrolment in Responding Boards	25
Figure 2.1	Distribution of Developmentally Challenged Pupils by Placement Setting: Ontario Public Boards	26
Figure 2.2	Distribution of Developmentally Challenged Pupils by Placement Setting: Ontario Separate Boards	26
Figure 2.3	Distribution of Behaviour-Disordered Pupils by Placement Setting: Ontario Public Boards	27
Figure 2.4	Distribution of Behaviour-Disordered Pupils by Placement Setting: Ontario Separate Boards	27
Figure 2.5A	Ontario Public Boards: Developmentally Challenged Median Prevalence According to Survey Responses	28
Figure 2.5B	Ontario Separate Boards: Developmentally Challenged Median Prevalence According to Survey Responses	28
Figure 2.6A	Ontario Public Boards: Behaviour Disordered Median Prevalence According to Survey Responses	29
Figure 2.6B	Ontario Separate Boards: Behaviour-Disordered Median Prevalence According to Survey Responses	29
Figure 2.7A	All Ontario Boards: Behaviour-Disordered Median Prevalence According to Survey Responses	30
Figure 2.7B	All Ontario Boards: Developmentally Challenged Median Prevalence According to Survey Responses	30
Figure 2.8	Ontario, United States, Europe, Japan: Prevalence of Developmentally Challenged	31
Figure 2.9	Ontario, United States, Europe, Japan: Prevalence of Behaviour Disordered	31

Section 3

Figure 3.1	Effect Size by Setting	46
Figure 3.2	Effect Size by Publication Status	47
Figure 3.3	Effect Size by Sampling Procedure	48
Figure 3.4	Effect Size by Mean Age	49
Figure 3.5	Effect Sizes for Academic Achievement Measures	50
Figure 3.6	Effect Sizes for Self-Concept Measures	51
Figure 3.7	Effect Sizes for Behavioural Observations Measures	52
Figure 3.8	Effect Sizes for Behavioural Rating Scales	53
Figure 3.9	Placement at Follow-up by Original Setting	54
Figure 3.10	Placement at Follow-up by Mean Age at Entry	55
Figure 3.11	Placement at Follow-up by Length of Follow-up	56
Figure 3.12	Placement at Follow-up by Country	57

Section 4

Table 4.1	Breakdown of School Boards in Ontario Focus Group Sample	63
Table 4.2	Major Themes Raised in the Focus Groups	71

Section 5

Figure 5.1	Effect Size by Setting	81
Figure 5.2	Effect Size by Sampling Procedure	81
Figure 5.3	Effect Size by Publication Status	83
Figure 5.4	Effect Size by Mean Age	83
Figure 5.5	Effect Sizes for Language Development Measures	84
Figure 5.6	Effect Sizes for Adaptive/Social Behaviour Measures	84
Figure 5.7	Effect Sizes for Motor Development Measures	85
Figure 5.8	Effect Sizes for Intellectual Development Measures	85

Section 6

Table 6.1	Breakdown of School Boards in Ontario Focus Group Sample	89
Table 6.2	Major Themes Raised in the Focus Groups	93

ACKNOWLEDGEMENTS

The investigators acknowledge
the careful and dedicated participation
of all the research assistants, especially

Barbara Brunhuber,
Anne Kerridge,
Martin Gervais,
Sabrina McTaggart,
and
Diana Shaffer.

About the Authors

Janice A. Leroux, Ph.D., principal investigator,
is an Associate Professor of Educational Studies
at the University of Ottawa. As a former elementary
school teacher and school principal, she has
over twenty years of experience across
all levels of education in Ontario.

Barry H. Schneider, Ph.D., co-investigator,
is an Associate Professor of Psychology at
the University of Ottawa and the Ontario Institute
for Studies in Education, Toronto. He has experience
in both clinical psychology and as a supervising
school psychologist in Ontario.

SOMMAIRE

La présente étude porte sur l'éducation des élèves présentant des anomalies du comportement ou des troubles du développement. Elle repose intégralement sur l'analyse scientifique de recherches effectuées dans ce domaine et sur les résultats d'une enquête menée auprès des autorités d'une douzaine de pays, de sept provinces et des Territoires du Nord-Ouest canadiens. Les réponses d'un nombre important de conseils scolaires ontariens ont également été examinées aux fins de cette enquête. Des groupes de réflexion ont été organisés dans plusieurs de ces conseils afin d'exposer le plus équitablement possible les vues des diverses parties intéressées et de donner une perspective provinciale valable en matière de placement et de programmation pour les deux groupes d'élèves à l'étude.

SURVOL DES POLITIQUES ET DES MODALITÉS EN VIGUEUR DANS LE MONDE

Les politiques en vigueur en matière d'éducation de l'enfance en difficulté sur la scène internationale, nationale et provinciale sont énoncées dans leurs grandes lignes et en particulier la philosophie actuelle et les modalités d'identification, de placement et d'évaluation courantes pour les élèves présentant des troubles du comportement ou des troubles du développement.

La majorité des pays étudiés sont favorables à l'élaboration d'une philosophie sous-jacente d'intégration des deux groupes d'enfants en difficulté dans le milieu scolaire traditionnel. Toutefois, la plupart de ces pays maintiennent un éventail d'options de placement et ne semblent avoir adopté des mesures concrètes qu'assez récemment en matière d'intégration. Le Danemark et la Finlande soulignent en particulier le souci de placer et de maintenir les enfants dans un milieu éducatif et social qui leur est familier. Par ailleurs, l'intégration de ces élèves dans des classes ordinaires est fortement recommandée ou du moins souhaitée par plusieurs des autorités compétentes.

Dans la plupart de ces pays, on reconnaît donc en substance le besoin d'aménager un ensemble cohérent et flexible de services spécialisés pour répondre aux besoins particuliers de l'enfance en difficulté. À cette fin, des dispositions précises sont prises. Ce sont, entre autres, des accords de collaboration avec d'autres agences en Australie et en Grande-Bretagne et une décentralisation des responsabilités et des services au Danemark. Certaines mesures complémentaires sont également envisagées telles des modifications aux installations ou l'amélioration des structures pédagogiques et
des services d'orientation, un apport d'équipement spécialisé et l'emploi de nouvelles technologies.

On note par ailleurs que la Suède fait figure de chef de file en matière d'intégration de l'enfance en difficulté. Ce pays endosse l'intégration des enfants en difficulté dans les classes ordinaires. On y dispense un enseignement individualisé adapté aux besoins de chaque élève. La nécessité de recourir le cas échéant à l'apprentissage en groupes dirigés et dans certains cas à des installations connexes est par conséquent acceptée. Tout le personnel enseignant reçoit en l'occurrence une formation pédagogique dans le domaine de l'enfance en difficulté.

Les États-Unis prévoient des procédures d'évaluation rigoureuses qui doivent permettre d'observer l'évolution sociale et le rendement scolaire de chaque élève. La plupart des autres pays soulignent plus ou moins explicitement l'importance de surveiller régulièrement ou de façon continue les progrès des élèves en difficulté dans le cadre de leur programme spécial individualisé.

Dans l'ensemble, une volonté de changement est exprimée clairement par la communauté internationale au regard de l'éducation de l'enfance en difficulté. La tendance générale semble, d'une part, encourager tout effort pertinent visant l'intégration des enfants en difficulté dans les milieux scolaires et, d'autre part, favoriser le maintien d'un réseau d'institutions spécialisées pour les enfants présentant des troubles du comportement ou des troubles du développement jugées sévères.

L'enquête révèle par ailleurs que les Pays-Bas, l'Allemagne et le Japon sont encore peu réceptifs à l'intégration. Les écoles spécialisées et les équipements collectifs constituent le recours privilégié de ces autorités pour le placement temporaire, voire permanent, des deux groupes d'élèves à l'étude.

Il convient d'indiquer également qu'un nombre restreint de pays jugent désirable la classification des élèves en difficulté et préfèrent préconiser un enseignement individualisé conçu en fonction des besoins particuliers de l'élève plutôt qu'en fonction de son anomalie. En revanche, l'identification diagnostique est courante, en particulier au Japon, pour déterminer le choix du placement de ces élèves.

Le Canada reconnaît progressivement les besoins de l'éducation de l'enfance en difficulté dans ses programmes d'enseignement. Un survol des modalités de placement indique que la majeure partie des répondants offrent un continuum d'options de placement pour les élèves présentant des troubles du comportement ou des troubles du développement. Le Nouveau-Brunswick a pour sa part adopté la philosophie de l'intégration et exige qu'un dossier appuie toute demande d'exclusion de la classe ordinaire. Les Territoires du Nord-Ouest préconisent également l'intégration et ont mis en place des mécanismes de soutien dans la communauté scolaire.

Le témoignage de la Colombie-Britannique résume bien les préoccupations canadiennes. Il s'agit en particulier de la mise en place d'une programmation spéciale et de services individualisés pertinents pour les deux groupes d'élèves à l'étude (plan d'enseignement individuel, personnel de soutien et personnel spécialisé, services de consultation, etc.). Par ailleurs, plusieurs provinces expriment le désir de ne pas classifier ces élèves aux fins de la programmation et d'éviter ainsi les désignations inutiles.

Quelques faits particuliers sont rapportés. L'Alberta recommande, par exemple, une identification précoce de l'enfance en difficulté; la Colombie-Britannique a mis en place des accords de financement interministériels pour mieux répondre aux besoins des enfants présentant des anomalies sévères; et les Territoires du Nord-Ouest favorisent l'acheminement de ressources vers les collectivités qui dispensent des programmes communautaires d'appoint.

Dans l'ensemble, les politiques respectives des provinces et des Territoires du Nord-Ouest ont tout lieu d'indiquer que la philosophie nationale à l'égard de l'enfance en difficulté est en mouvance et qu'elles favorisent de plus en plus l'intégration.

Les réponses des conseils scolaires ontariens varient en précision et en complétude. Quelques conseils ont cependant élaboré, de leur propre initiative, soit une politique solide d'intégration dans les classes ordinaires, soit des mécanismes précis d'évaluation, soit un modèle de services pour répondre aux besoins des enfants présentant des anomalies du comportement ou des troubles du développement.

Une analyse comparative permet de placer l'Ontario dans le contexte international. L'Ontario fait partie du groupe de répondants qui permettent une certaine flexibilité quant au placement des enfants en difficulté. La classification des élèves en difficulté aux fins de la programmation est enchâssée dans la philosophie et la loi ontarienne contrairement, par exemple, aux Territoires du Nord-Ouest canadiens. À l'instar des autres autorités canadiennes, l'évaluation est effectuée au niveau du programme spécial individualisé de l'élève en difficulté.

COMPARAISON DES TAUX DE PRÉVALENCE PAR RÉGION

L'étude révèle le nombre d'élèves identifiés comme présentant des troubles du comportement ou des troubles du développement en Ontario, aux États-Unis, en Europe et au Japon. Cette étape de l'enquête vise à représenter graphiquement les variations qui existent à travers ces régions. Les données des conseils scolaires ontariens d'écoles publiques et séparées ont été traitées parallèlement afin de permettre la comparaison des effectifs d'élèves en difficulté dans chaque système scolaire. Des diagrammes en bâtons illustrent également la répartition des élèves des deux groupes à l'étude selon leur placement dans les classes ordinaires, les classes pour élèves en difficulté et les écoles pour élèves en difficulté.

On note que la proportion d'élèves identifiés comme présentant des troubles du comportement ou des troubles du développement varie de manière considérable entre les conseils scolaires ontariens. En même temps, des fluctuations importantes au niveau du placement de ces élèves sont exposées dans les deux systèmes scolaires.

De manière générale, les taux de prévalence ontariens et mondiaux ne suffisent pas à expliquer les différences qui existent dans chaque région en matière de modalités de placement. Il convient pourtant de souligner que le nombre de cas enregistré par chacune des autorités est intimement lié aux facteurs qui influencent leurs modalités de placement comme le degré de tolérance envers un comportement jugé atypique et les conditions sociales, économiques et politiques du milieu. C'est pourquoi une comparaison de l'ensemble de ces taux de prévalence, à partir des représentations graphiques, doit être effectuée avec prudence.

À toutes fins utiles, on note que les taux ontariens de prévalence se situent en général entre ceux des États-Unis et ceux de l'Europe.

Analyse des coûts et ententes contractuelles en Ontario
La plupart des conseils scolaires ne disposent pas de données quant à l'analyse des coûts au regard des deux groupes d'élèves en difficulté.

Des ententes contractuelles ont été passées entre quelques conseils scolaires ontariens et des organismes gouvernementaux, en particulier le ministère des Services sociaux et communautaires, le ministère de la Santé et le ministère des Services correctionnels. Le plus grand nombre d'ententes concernent les élèves présentant des troubles du comportement.

Personnel de soutien en Ontario
Une énumération exhaustive du personnel de soutien disponible dans la province pour servir les deux groupes d'élèves en difficulté ne permet pas d'évaluer la qualité des services dispensés. Il semble cependant que les conseils scolaires du Nord de l'Ontario et les conseils scolaires ruraux se heurtent à de longues listes d'attente ou n'ont pas accès à certains de ces services.

Comparaison des définitions canadiennes et internationales
On a demandé aux répondants de définir ce qu'ils entendaient par «troubles du développement» et «troubles du comportement».

La plupart d'entre eux associent la formule «troubles du développement» à l'idée d'un retard du développement intellectuel, d'où l'emploi d'expressions telles «déficience mentale», «arriération mentale» ou «handicap mental». On note cependant que l'utilisation du quotient intellectuel (Q.I) n'est plus courante pour symboliser ce retard. Des troubles du développement au milieu social et le fait de ne pas bénéficier normalement du programme commun d'enseignement caractérisent pour plusieurs cette anomalie.

Plusieurs thèmes reviennent dans les définitions de «troubles du comportement». Ce sont entre autres : le fait d'un comportement anormal dans une situation normale qui se traduit le plus souvent par l'action conjuguée de l'agressivité, de l'inhibition, de la peur ou de la dépression; l'incapacité de nouer et d'entretenir des relations personnelles; et un comportement qui altère le rendement scolaire et perturbe les autres élèves.

Il est difficile de juger jusqu'à quel point ces définitions justifient les taux d'identification enregistrés dans chaque région pour les élèves présentant des troubles du développement ou des troubles du comportement. Des études de cas détaillées sont présentées ultérieurement à des groupes de réflexion afin de développer une base commune de discusions dans la province sur le thème de l'identification, du placement et de l'évaluation de ces élèves.

MILIEU D'ENSEIGNEMENT OPTIMAL POUR LES ÉLÈVES PRÉSENTANT DES TROUBLES DE COMPORTEMENT OU DES TROUBLES DU DÉVELOPPEMENT

Existe-t-il un milieu d'enseignement optimal pour les élèves présentant des troubles du comportement ou des développement? Cette question est examinée ici à la lumière des recherches menées dans ce domaine depuis les années 60.

Les auteurs devaient d'abord choisir une méthode d'analyse comparative qui leur permettrait de tirer profit de l'ensemble des recherches. Toute étude comparative de groupes de recherches présente en soi des obstacles. Celle-ci a cependant soulevé d'autres problèmes. D'une part, peu de chercheurs ont eu la possibilité de travailler avec des groupes équivalents d'élèves en difficulté pour offrir une comparaison valable des différents milieux d'enseignement. D'autre part, ils ont rarement tenu compte de l'interdépendance de facteurs tels le milieu, le programme et le personnel enseignant. De plus, la nature complexe de l'évolution sociale et intellectuelle chez les deux groupes d'élèves, conjuguée à l'absence d'une terminologie standard ainsi qu'à l'utilisation de variables, de mesures et de tests différents selon les recherches, ont rendu difficile l'analyse de cette documentation.

En l'occurrence, une stratégie dite «méta-analytique» a été choisie pour effectuer l'étude comparative des différents groupes de recherches. La stratégie en question semble offrir l'avantage de mieux conserver le caractère spécifique de chaque étude et de permettre par conséquent une interprétation plus acceptable des résultats. Les recherches de suivi ont fait l'objet d'une étude distincte dans le but d'évaluer les programmes spéciaux sur une période prolongée.

Par ailleurs, la méthode de «la preuve la plus convaincante» (Best evidence analysis), qui consiste à isoler les résultats des recherches les mieux conçues, a été utilisée de préférence à celle qui imposait l'analyse du nombre considérable de recherches disponibles dans ce domaine dont les résultats pourraient être plus discutables.

Les études choisies ont répondu aux trois critères suivants :
1. Représenter le mieux possible la population des élèves présentant soit des troubles du comportement, soit des troubles du développement, et être menée dans au moins un des milieux d'enseignement où évolue chacune de ces populations;
2. Permettre la comparaison des changements survenus entre les élèves du groupe expérimental et ceux, d'âge similaire, du groupe-témoin; et
3. a) Rendre compte des changements apparents au niveau du rendement scolaire, du comportement et du concept de soi des élèves présentant des troubles du comportement; et
b) Rendre compte de tels changements au niveau du développement cognitif, moteur et de la capacité d'adaptation des élèves présentant des troubles du développement.

Ces études ont ensuite été soumises à l'examen de plusieurs facteurs qualitatifs et quantitatifs, entre autres, la description diagnostique et le quotient intellectuel (Q.I.) des sujets, l'origine des données, l'expérience du personnel enseignant, la répartition des sexes, la taille de l'échantillon, etc.

Les résultats de l'étude, illustrés au moyen de diagrammes en bâtons doivent, pour de nombreuses raisons dont celles expliquées plus haut, être interprétés avec extrême prudence.

Conclusions : Élèves présentant des troubles du comportement
Certaines observations tacites peuvent être faites pour les enfants présentant des troubles du comportement. Ces élèves ont besoin d'un appui plus important que celui dispensé actuellement dans les classes ordinaires par des enseignantes ou des enseignants non assistés. Les salles-ressources semblent élever le concept de soi chez ces élèves. Un appui continu et prolongé leur est le plus souvent indispensable. Les recherches de suivi indiquent que les programmes spéciaux ne semblent pas en général offrir à ces élèves la chance de réintégrer entièrement les classes ordinaires et de poursuivre normalement le programme commun d'enseignement.

Les résultats ne permettent pas de clarifier de façon significative la question du choix de programmes pour les élèves présentant des troubles du comportement. En l'absence de données plus précises, le principe du placement le moins restrictif possible devrait être appliqué.

Conclusions : Élèves présentant des troubles du développement
La recherche supporte clairement l'intégration des élèves présentant des troubles du développement modérées (identifiés en Ontario comme _élèves déficients moyens_) dans le milieu scolaire traditionnel. Elle ne permet cependant pas de déterminer si l'un ou l'autre des milieux d'enseignement étudiés pourrait être qualifié de milieu d'enseignement _optimal_. La classe ordinaire ne peut pas par exemple être considérée comme un placement adéquat pour l'ensemble de ces élèves étant donné qu'ils présentent une diversité de troubles fonctionnels et du comportement plus ou moins sévères.

La planification de l'enseignement bénéficierait considérablement de données scientifiques plus complètes dans les deux domaines. La recherche devrait à l'avenir offrir une description exhaustive des milieux d'enseignement, des programmes dispensés, du profil des élèves et du personnel enseignant en vue de permettre de tirer des conclusions déterminables. En attendant, il est crucial d'évaluer chaque programme avec prudence et de suivre les progrès des élèves présentant des troubles du comportement ou des troubles du développement sur une base individuelle.

PERSPECTIVE PROVINCIALE EN MATIÈRE DE PLACEMENT ET DE PROGRAMMATION

Deux séries d'entretiens avec des groupes de réflexion organisés dans toutes les régions de la province ont permis de faire le point sur l'éducation des enfants présentant des troubles du comportement ou des troubles du développement en Ontario.

Ces groupes se composaient de cadres scolaires, d'enseignantes et d'enseignants et de parents représentant les systèmes scolaires publics et séparés.

Les trois étapes suivantes ont été suivies pour chaque série d'entretiens.

Étape I   **Mise en situation.**
Il s'agissait dans un premier temps d'explorer les politiques, les modalités de placement et les plans des conseils scolaires sélectionnés.

Deux études de cas fictives ont été présentées aux cadres scolaires et au personnel enseignant qui devaient ensuite décrire les modalités de placement et d'évaluation applicables pour chaque cas. Les deux études proposées devaient être dignes de crédibilité mais poser en même temps un dilemme quant au choix du placement le plus approprié pour l'élève en difficulté.

Étape II   **Entretiens de suivi.**
Tous les participants ont été invités à élucider leurs réponses et à exposer toute réflexion ou question pertinentes au cours d'entretiens semi-structurés. Pour leur part, les parents d'élèves en difficulté ont été invités à réagir aux modalités en vigueur dans le conseil scolaire de leur région. Des questionnaires ont été élaborés pour chaque groupe de réflexion afin de guider et d'animer ces entretiens.

Étape III   **Corroboration des déclarations.**
Un entretien téléphonique entre un membre de la faculté d'administration d'Ottawa et un cadre supérieur de chaque conseil scolaire a permis de confirmer l'ensemble des témoignages recueillis et de déterminer quelles conséquences aurait une compression des dépenses sur la programmation spéciale en Ontario.

Voici en bref les conclusions de la transcription intégrale des deux séries d'entretiens.

Conclusions : Élèves présentant des troubles du comportement

Étude de cas 1 - Résumé : Jack, 8 ans, est en 3e année. Il a changé d'école sept fois depuis la maternelle. Il s'emporte facilement et se mêle fréquemment aux bagarres. En classe, il est impulsif et provoquant. L'intelligence de Jack est normale ou supérieure à celle de ses camarades. Jack et sa jeune soeur sont élevés par leur père. Ils ont des contacts irréguliers avec leur mère.

Étude de cas 2 - Résumé : Jenny, 14 ans, redouble sa 8e année. Ses absences sont chroniques. Elle est effacée et silencieuse en classe et se désintéresse de son travail scolaire bien qu'elle ne semble pas avoir de problèmes d'apprentissage évidents. Jenny ne reçoit pas de services de consultation malgré les recommandations de l'école.

La majorité des participants estiment que la classe ordinaire est un milieu d'enseignement privilégié pour des élèves présentant des troubles modérés du comportement comme Jack et Jenny à la condition qu'un appui adéquat leur soit offert.

Le nombre croissant de problèmes associés aux troubles du comportement dans les écoles ontariennes inquiète les populations francophone et anglophone, rurale comme urbaine. Quel appui peut en l'occurrence être considéré adéquat pour répondre aux besoins particuliers de ces élèves? Les déclarations, à quelques exceptions près, sont unanimes.

Les élèves présentant des troubles du comportement requièrent sur une base continue un enseignement amélioré et des soins de qualité dans un milieu scolaire plus ouvert à l'intégration.

Le personnel enseignant, le personnel d'appui et les cadres scolaires ont besoin de recevoir une formation pédagogique accrue qui leur permettna de s'occuper quotidiennement des besoins particuliers de ces élèves.

Les organismes gouvernementaux doivent redoubler d'attention envers les familles et leur offrir des services soutenus dans leurs commnunautés et si besoin est dans leur foyer. Par ailleurs, les familles et l'école doivent entretenir des relations suivies qui leur permettront de partager le plus normalement possible la responsabilité de l'éducation de ces enfants. Une meilleure compréhension de la philosophie et des modalités d'identification, de placement et d'évaluation sont indispensables à l'ouverture d'un dialogue entre l'école et la famille.

Toutes les régions de la province devraient avoir accès aux services et à la programmation spéciale et ce, depuis les années de formation jusqu'aux années de spécialisation. Des normes provinciales sont nécessaires à cette fin. Il importe également que ces normes décrivent les buts de cette programmation spéciale individualisée et garantissent en même temps le maintien des qualités inhérentes à la classe ordinaire et à l'école.

De telles normes devraient par ailleurs offrir une certaine flexibilité. Les conseils scolaires locaux doivent en effet pouvoir prendre des dispositions raisonnables pour tenir compte du degré

tolérance manifesté dans leur région envers des comportements jugés atypiques sans toutefois compromettre l'égalité d'accès aux services et aux programmes spéciaux individualisés.

Les conseils scolaires dont les ressources sont limitées tels certains conseils ruraux, ceux du Nord et ceux qui dispensent une éducation en langue française, pourraient envisager le partage d'équipes de spécialistes itinérants et expérimentés dans l'identification des problèmes du comportement et le suivi des élèves présentant des troubles du comportement. De telles initiatives pourraient permettre à ces conseils de se conformer aux normes provinciales.

Le développement d'une programmation optimale pour ces élèves est indispensable. La création d'un centre de recherches dont le personnel serait hautement qualifié et expérimenté répondrait à ce besoin. Une telle installation pourrait également faciliter le partage des ressources pédagogiques et la formation permanente du personnel enseignant et du personnel de soutien.

Toutes les parties intéressées reconnaissent que la programmation spéciale individualisée peut répondre adéquatement aux besoins des élèves présentant des troubles du comportement. Toutefois, la majorité des cadres supérieurs des conseils scolaires soutiennent que la qualité d'une telle programmation serait gravement compromise en période de compression des dépenses. Ils admettent qu'une réduction en personnel de soutien survient généralement en pareille circonstance.

Conclusions : Élèves présentant des troubles du développement

Étude 1 - Résumé : Tina, 7 ans, est la cadette d'une famille de trois enfants dont la mère célibataire travaille. Ses habiletés langagières et son apprentissage de l'autonomie se développent lentement depuis l'âge de 3 ans. Ses capacités motrices semblent être bonnes. La mère de Tina insiste pour obtenir l'intégration de sa fille dans une classe ordinaire. Une évaluation psychologique indique que Tina est déficiente moyenne.

Étude 2 - Résumé : Markus, un garçon athlétique de 14 ans, est trisomique. Son habileté à se prendre en charge est raisonnable. Il compte jusqu'à 100 et est capable de lire des phrases simples. Il a besoin d'évoluer dans un milieu d'enseignement structuré sinon il devient indifférent et désorganisé. L'écart entre son rendement scolaire et celui de ses camarades va grandissant. Une évaluation psychologique indique que Markus est déficient moyen.

La majorité des enseignantes et des enseignants estiment que Tina bénéficierait d'un placement dans une classe ordinaire pendant quelques années. Markus, plus âgé, ne pourrait en revanche satisfaire aux exigences de l'enseignement secondaire. Plus tard, Tina devra également être placée dans un milieu d'enseignement spécialisé comme la classe pour élèves en difficulté. La même recommandation est faite pour des élèves déficients qui présentent des troubles fonctionnels ou du comportement plus sévères.

Deux visions de l'éducation des élèves troubles du développement coexistent dans la province. L'une soutient une programmation optimale axée sur un apprentissage de l'autonomie et des soins thérapeutiques suivis. L'autre favorise l'intégration des élèves déficients moyens dans la communauté scolaire traditionnelle. Un grand nombre de familles voient dans l'intégration la chance de développer les habiletés et les aptitudes de leurs enfants dans une ambiance normale et chaleureuse suceptible de générer chez eux l'estime de soi, la satisfaction personnelle et la considération des autres.

Ces deux visions ne sont pas contradictoires. Cependant, l'accès aux services spécialisés dont bénéficient les écoles pour élèves en difficulté reste encore restreint dans les écoles traditionnelles. La justification des coûts de lancement d'une programmation idéale qui exigerait le maintien de services spécialisés semble être en partie responsable de cette carence. Il convient de rappeler pourtant que de tels coûts sont reconnus pour être élevés. Par ailleurs, la recherche n'a pas prouvé que les écoles pour élèves en difficulté sont une avenue plus économique pour le système scolaire ou plus profitable pour les élèves en question.

En l'occurrence, l'intégration des élèves troubles du développement dans l'école traditionnelle, souhaitée par un nombre important de parents, pourrait être viable. Il s'agirait en particulier de maximiser l'emploi des ressources, d'investir dans la formation intensive du personnel et dans de meilleurs modèles de services.

Par ailleurs, des modalités d'évaluation plus détaillées et plus complètes sont nécessaires aux fins de la programmation spéciale et de l'obligation de rendre des comptes. Une ouverture du dialogue est cruciale si l'on veut permettre aux élèves déficients moyens de se réaliser pleinement.

ORGANIZATION OF THE REPORT

The legal status of special education programs in Ontario changed radically with the advent of mandated special education in 1985. In 1990, the Ministry of Education requested a review of policies, placement practices, and plans of selected school boards with regard to two groups of exceptional pupils — those identified as having behaviour disorders and the developmentally challenged. This report contains:

1. a review of policies in twelve countries, seven Canadian provinces, and twenty-nine Ontario school boards;

2. a survey of the prevalence of behaviour-disordered and developmentally challenged pupils, according to figures provide by survey respondents;

3. a review of research on optimal educational environments for pupils with behaviour disorders;

4. a review of the policies, placement practices, and plans for pupils identified as behaviour disordered in Ontario;

5. a review of research on optimal education for developmentally challenged pupils; and

6. a review of the policies, placement practices, and plans for pupils identified as developmentally challenged in Ontario.

SECTION 1

AN INTERNATIONAL SURVEY OF POLICIES AND PROCEDURES

ABSTRACT

This section reviews and summarizes the placement philosophies, policies, options, and evaluations for behaviour-disordered and developmentally challenged students in twelve countries, Canadian provinces, and Ontario school boards. Five research questions were devised to gather information concerning the placement and evaluation of these students:

- *What is the placement philosophy of the jurisdiction for these exceptionalities?*
- *What placement policies have been developed for these exceptionalities?*
- *What placement options are available for these exceptionalities?*
- *What placement procedures for these exceptionalities are used?*
- *What procedures are in place for identifying these exceptionalities, specifying individual programming needs, and evaluating pupil progress?*

Jurisdictions vary widely in their emphasis on categorization of exceptionalities, with some insisting on a non-categorical approach. Ontario is one of the locations in which categories are a fundamental feature of legislation and program planning.

Educational jurisdictions around the world have adopted a range of policies with regard to the placement of exceptional students. In order to provide an external perspective on Ontario's provisions for behaviour-disordered and developmentally challenged pupils, policy documents provided by educational authorities in twelve countries, and by departments and Ministries of Education in seven provinces and one territory of Canada were reviewed, along with those provided by a sample of 29 Ontario school boards. Throughout this report we use the terms "behaviour disorder" and "developmental challenge". However, we have included information from outside Ontario based on materials in which synonymous or overlapping terms and definitions were used. These related terms include "emotionally disturbed", "conduct disordered", and "socially maladjusted", in the case of the behaviour disordered. The scope of the sections on developmental challenge is limited to youngsters whose developmental handicaps are moderate. These youngsters were referred to as "trainable mentally retarded" in previous Ontario legislation, and as "moderately mentally retarded" in many medical texts. The documents obtained were scanned for responses to five research questions concerning the placement and evaluation of students with behavioural disorders and developmental challenge:

1. What is the philosophy underlying provision of educational environments for these exceptionalities?
2. What placement policies have been developed for these exceptionalities?
3. What placement options are available for these pupils?
4. What placement procedures for these exceptionalities are used?
5. What evaluation procedures are in place for programs and/or pupil progress?

Respondents were also asked to indicate the numbers of pupils who had been identified under these categories; these enrolment data are presented in Section 2.

Policies in Other Countries

Questionnaires were sent in June 1990 to educational authorities in countries whose economic resources and literacy rates were similar to those of Ontario. Responses were received from 12 countries: Australia, Belgium, Denmark, Finland, Germany, Ireland, Japan, the Netherlands, Sweden, Switzerland, the United Kingdom, and the United States. In most cases, the respondent had prepared a detailed written response explaining the country's policies within the context of its own education law and demographic characteristics. Many of these letters commented on recent trends and changes. The following capsule summaries abstract the answers to the five questions indicated above for purposes of comparison. It is obviously beyond the scope of this document to describe the educational systems of each country more generally. The responses received vary considerably in detail. The terminology used in the original documents varies in its apparent equivalence to Canadian usage. Therefore, we are able to provide a more comprehensive description of provisions in some countries than in others. Documents in English, French, and German were analyzed directly. Synopses rather than full translations were used for documents in other languages.

Australia

Much of the responsibility for education in Australia lies with state authorities. The Commonwealth Government does provide some special funding for special education programs and special education services. Subsequent enquiries resulted in responses from four Australian states (New South Wales, Queensland, Tasmania, and Western Australia) and from the Northern Territory. These were among the most articulate and complete documents received from any jurisdiction, and dealt with many aspects of the education of pupils experiencing the two disabilities under consideration. Issues addressed included the interface of prevention and intervention, responsibilities of regular classroom teachers for these children, and the process of negotiation – described as such – for additional services and/or alternative learning environments.

Placement Philosophy. Philosophies included "label free" categorization of students, with mainstreaming as a goal and provision of special services based on individual program needs rather than a description of disabilities. Most of the Australian documents explicitly endorse a "cascade" model of service delivery. It is expected that special education services be delivered in "the least restrictive environment possible" (e.g., Western Australia Ministry of Education, 1984).

Placement Policies. State Departments of Education provide guidelines for local school districts, which have the primary responsibility for educational interventions in special education. Policies in each district must reflect the state policies for services, placements, and programs. Mainstreaming and integration of students wherever possible were reported. Responses received from two states highlighted collaborative arrangements with other agencies for coordinated services. As indicated above, the documents provide very full detail as to the expectations of the regular school, though they do not preclude referral to special schools should regular-school provisions prove insufficient.

Placement Options. While the regular school is expected to make very thorough efforts to accommodate pupils with special needs, this philosophy does not exclude more restrictive environments such as special schools. A range of options was indicated, though it is clearly not expected that each school district provide the full continuum of settings; many do not. "Special units" (e.g., self-contained classes in ordinary schools) are also available in many schools. Implementation of the "cascade" model results in constant fluctuations in the enrolments of special schools and special units, which is considered acceptable. A "supportive school model" coordinates many levels of a total school program for exceptional students in Tasmania. In Queensland, services are described as needs-based and child-centred, focusing on: (1) "alternative curriculum for those whose educational needs exceed the capacity for regular education"; and (2) "supported curriculum for those whose educational needs require curriculum modification or alternative strategies or methodology". These models were described in considerable detail, and appear to have been designed to ensure the viability of the "least restrictive" option regardless of whether a more self-contained placement option is available in the child's community.

Placement Procedures. The Northern Territory places students based on a description of learning skills and assets, not just on the category of exceptionality identified. Queensland uses Individual Educational Plans (IEPs) to provide for special needs in a continuum of programs and locations. There appears to be very heavy emphasis on programming. Pupil identification and placement procedures were not well described in the documents. We infer that these are less formal than those mandated in Ontario.

Evaluation Procedures. A placement and review panel meets at regular intervals in the Northern Territory in order to monitor students' progress. In the other Australian responses, emphasis was placed on the continuous review of IEPs, frequently at the school level.

Belgium

Documents received from the French-speaking sector of the Belgian educational system indicated a classification system for exceptionalities based on severity and nature of handicap. A multidisciplinary assessment is mandated for placement decisions, although very specific identification criteria are specified for French-speaking schools nationwide. The mandated assessment procedures for the behaviour-disordered emphasize the specification of both an academic/intellectual and behavioural/emotional profile for each child. Special schools are the usual placement for pupils with both severe behavioural difficulties and developmental challenges, though integration seems to be encouraged for other categories of exceptionality. However, the Ministry official was aware of very few cases in which pupils with these two exceptionalities are being accommodated in regular schools.

Denmark

In 1980 legislation was passed mandating a principle of normalization of the conditions of the handicapped.

Placement Philosophy. Three fundamental principles guide educational provisions for the handicapped:
- normalization
- decentralization
- integration

Normalization, according to the documents received, implies putting the handicapped on an equal footing with all other citizens with regard to laws, administration, and political authorities. Normalization is seen as "a challenge to society, not a wish or a demand for 'adapting' the individual to make him 'normal' ". *Decentralization* involves the transfer, from the state to the local level of jurisdiction, of the responsibility for administrative structures, which would be large enough to ensure a satisfactory level of service, yet small enough to establish a "real grass roots democracy".

Integration is a principle that is promoted indirectly from legislation. A parliamentary resolution in 1969 states that "the primary and lower secondary school should be expanded so as to provide for the teaching of handicapped pupils, to the greatest possible extent, in an ordinary school environment" (Danish Ministry of Education, 1986, p. 11). Prior to that, pupils with very severe problems were the responsibility not of local school authorities, but of the national government.

The Danish Ministry of Education cites five principles to guide the placement of exceptional students:
- Proximity: the child should attend school as close to home as possible.
- As little intervention as possible: the child should be offered no more special support than absolutely necessary.
- Integration: instruction of the handicapped child should take place in an ordinary and normal school environment if at all possible.
- Efficiency: measures must be taken to ensure that the program provided enables the child to maximally achieve his/her potential.
- Motivation: it is considered essential that the special education program specified, including the degree of integration, be congruent with both teachers' and parents' beliefs as to what is suitable for the child in question.

This philosophy was articulated with considerable emotion. For example, the Ministry document specified that the social welfare system in effect from 1930 to the 1960s provided for the material, but not the human needs, of handicapped individuals. Society "bought out" its responsibilities to them by providing pensions or special institutions, in exchange for the segregation of these individuals. The current policy, made possible by "progress, optimism, and prosperity" (p.9), provided for greater inclusion of handicapped individuals in "normal human activity". The changes apply to pupils with both intellectual and emotional/behavioural exceptionalities. However, provisions for the developmentally challenged are more widely discussed.

Placement Policies. In Denmark, schools are required to provide special instruction and other special educational assistance for pupils whose development requires special support. Special educational assistance consists of:
- special instruction, to provide for optimum individual achievement
- stimulation and training, to reduce physical or psychological dysfunction as much as possible
- counselling and guidance, in order to instruct the child's parents and teachers in the best ways of dealing with the child's needs
- educational aids, employing technology to reduce the adverse impact of the handicap on the child's learning

Placement Options. Primary and secondary schools provide special assistance ranging from totally integrated special instruction in the regular class to totally segregated special instruction in special boarding schools. Thus, while integration into regular schools is strongly advocated, there still exist a small number of completely self-contained facilities. The extent of assistance may vary from one-half or one lesson per week for a few weeks to the entire instruction during the course of schooling, meaning full-time special provisions without any unassisted participation in regular school or class activity.

Placement Procedures. Placement procedures include a process of evaluation, taking into consideration the wishes of teachers, the parents, and the child. Evaluation procedures are not detailed in the documents. However, the local school personnel appear to be extensively involved in the initial placement decisions. Parents clearly have the right to appeal.

Evaluation Procedures. Specific procedures for the assessment of pupils' needs and of their programs were not specified in the documents received. However, the documents emphasized the need for evaluating each individual child's functioning in each educational and social domain. Inferences based on diagnostic labels were explicitly discouraged.

Finland

In Finland, according to the Comprehensive School Act of 1983, special education is provided for any pupil who is so badly handicapped or retarded that she/he cannot cope with the instruction of a comprehensive school, or who, because of emotional disorders, has special needs. Until now developmentally challenged pupils have been the responsibility of the central government. However, plans are underway to transfer this obligation to local school councils, who administer special education to all other pupils in need.

Placement Philosophy. The Finnish system of service delivery is based on a philosophy of local autonomy within the constraints of national legislation. This legislation does not provide for the classification of exceptionalities, though statistics are compiled by exceptionality. The municipality decides on the arrangement of special education according to the regulations of the school system, taking into account the pupils' needs.

Placement Policies. The documents indicate that students should be placed in the least restrictive setting possible. It is expected that pupils receive special assistance close to their homes. These policies are presented as guidelines from the national government to the local authorities, who seem to have considerable discretion in implementing them. Municipalities must arrange special education as "an integral part of general education".

Placement Options. The first alternative is to integrate the pupil into general education. The student may be given special instruction individually or in small groups. If this alternative is not appropriate, a number of other alternatives may be adopted, including arranging for instruction in a special group, class, or school. A municipality "may arrange part of [a pupil's] special education in the state-funded special schools for the aurally, visually, and physically handicapped". Presumably, a number of developmentally challenged pupils are enrolled in these. The documents also mention the possibility of special education within hospitals and treatment centres. If a municipality elects to provide special education within such centres, it must locate a treatment facility within its boundaries.

Placement Procedures. The Finnish National Board of General Education provides guidelines on the arrangement of special education, and the municipal school board makes the placement decisions. The National Board suggests that the school board should take the opinions of parents and experts into consideration when making placement decisions. Evaluation procedures were not specified in the documents received.

Germany

The German educational system features considerable provincial autonomy, though there are increased efforts to coordinate provincial services. Special schools for exceptional pupils have been a tradition in German special education, although enrolment in these special schools has been generally dropping in recent years. However, the response received indicates that this trend is not evident in either of the specific instances of the behaviourally disordered or the developmentally challenged. Special education is required for mentally handicapped students if their cognitive and emotional deficiencies are considerable. The aim of special education provisions for the behaviour disordered is to ensure the return of the student to the normal school as soon as possible. Placement in special schools normally requires the opinion of an expert consultant and participation of the parents. These individuals are also involved in regular reviews in order to determine whether the special school placement is still necessary.

Great Britain

The Education Act 1981 specified that special educational provisions should be based on the special educational needs of individual children, with a focus on the child's individual needs, rather than on global inferences about the requirements of her/his disability.

Placement Philosophy. The operative principle is that all children for whom the Local Educational Authority (LEA) decides to provide special education are "to be educated in ordinary schools, so far as is reasonably possible, and are to associate in the activities of the school with other children".

Placement Options. Different patterns of provisions are available. These include resource provisions in ordinary schools, extensive links between special and ordinary schools, and special needs support services. While the nature of the links between special and ordinary schools were not detailed in the documents received, we assume that these consist of joint educational and recreational activity, as well as, possibly, partial enrolment in each.

Placement Procedures. The LEAs are legally required to specify in detail the special educational provision that they consider appropriate for the special educational needs of individual children. Specifications must include facilities and equipment, staffing arrangements, teaching methods and approaches, and, where relevant, educational environment and access. The LEA must describe the type of school it considers appropriate for the child, and should in principle comply with parental preferences in school admissions. Close consultation with the Social Services Department is required in reaching decisions on the special educational provisions and placements for children in care or under supervision.

Evaluation Procedures. The Department of Education specifies that continuous monitoring of the child's progress must be undertaken. This monitoring requires that distinctions be made between:

- the child's past and present levels of functioning, emotional states, and interests;
- the analysis of the child's consequent learning difficulties; the specification of goals for change in the child and the environment;
- the specification of the child's requirement for different kinds of approaches, facilities, or resources and any modifications required; the perceptions and wishes of the parent and child; and
- the special educational provision and services required to meet the identified needs.

Ireland

The Special Education Section of the Ministry of Education indicated in their response that the designation of "moderately mentally handicapped" was used in Ireland to refer to the population designated elsewhere as "trainable". Most of these pupils attend one of 14 special schools. There are also a small number attending special classes in ordinary schools.

Behaviour-disordered students are not defined as clearly as the other categories of exceptionality, for several reasons. The Ministry respondent indicated that such a global label would encompass too wide a range of difficulties to be meaningful and useful. He also believed that there would be very extensive overlap between such a category and the other exceptionalities that are identified (e.g., intellectual, communications). Despite the lack of formal identification, special schools do exist for youngsters with behaviour disorders of serious degree. Special guidance centres are operated by local health authorities for pupils whose behaviour problems are less severe; these are only available in the larger population centres. Pupils may attend these centres on a withdrawal basis. Others may attend full time for short periods of crisis. In addition, "Youth Encounter Projects" are aimed at young people who have become seriously alienated from the conventional school system or who have been involved in minor delinquent acts. There are four small projects of this nature in the Republic of Ireland.

A "white paper" was issued in 1980 advocating increased integration, though without abandoning the segregated classes and schools. Nevertheless, local schools are not required by law to have any special provision for youngsters with exceptional educational needs.

Japan

Placement Philosophy. Handicapped children should have special support services and need to have education appropriate to their handicapping condition and individual stage of development. While individual differences in the degree and manifestations of disorders are recognized, the documents obtained from Japan reflect a strong commitment to typologies of exceptionality. Placement is largely determined by diagnostic category and degree of severity. This contrasts sharply with the emphasis on individual needs profiles and decentralization in many of the documents received from Europe and Australia.

Placement Options. Special education is provided in special schools and in special classes in ordinary elementary and lower secondary schools in Japan. There are three types of special schools: schools for the blind, schools for the deaf, and schools for the handicapped, including schools for the mentally retarded,* for the physically handicapped, and for the health impaired. For mildly handicapped children, special classes are established in ordinary elementary and lower secondary schools as required. Special classes are further divided into specific types, including special classes for the mentally handicapped, and classes for the emotionally disturbed.

Youngsters whose developmental challenges are moderate or severe are educated in special self-contained schools. Pupils whose developmental changes are considered mild, but who also "particularly lack social adaptability", are enrolled in these special schools as well. Instruction is provided in a small-group setting. At the elementary level, emphasis is on acquiring basic life skills and participating in group activities. At the lower secondary level, instruction is provided with emphasis on the acquisition of the necessary attitude and knowledge for vocational life and for social independence.

Education placements for children with "problem behaviours" is provided in ordinary classes. Educational methods such as counselling and play therapy are used. Children whose emotional problems are severe are provided with instruction at an educational guidance office, or child guidance centre, or are educated in special classes for the emotionally disturbed.*

Placement Procedures. Municipal boards of education give guidance on appropriate educational placement for children with special educational needs. They identify and evaluate handicapped children based on the results of medical examinations for school entrance and other data. The boards establish Advisory Committees on Educational Placements composed of doctors, teachers, staff of child welfare facilities, and other specialists. These boards also provide guidance on educational placement in special classes in ordinary elementary and lower secondary schools. Evaluation procedures are not specified in the documents received. There is no mention of parent involvement in placement decisions. There is considerable weight assigned to the recommendations of professionals, especially medical practitioners.

---

* Terminology used in original documents

The Netherlands

Placement Philosophy. The Netherlands have established separate schools, recognize 15 different exceptionalities, and do not espouse mainstreaming as a general practice. However, the Interim Act of 1985 is "designed in such a way as to encourage the eventual crossing over of pupils from special education to normal education" and to "improve the ability of ordinary schools to cater to a wide range of educational needs".

Since the 1970s policy has emerged that focuses on increasing the help given children with learning difficulties by ordinary schools. Nevertheless, special schools appear to be a well-established feature of Dutch special education, according to the Ministry of Education's 1989 documents, and would appear to be the usual placement for youngsters with behaviour disorders and developmental challenges.

Placement Options. As noted above, the 1000 special schools are the major mode of service delivery. However, since the Interim Act emphasizes interaction between exceptional and non-exceptional pupils, several new services have been introduced. These include peripatetic supervision, which entails assistance provided by teachers from the special school to pupils and teachers in regular schools, and split placement or part-time attendance, i.e., allowing a pupil registered in a special school to attend regular school part time. The latter is becoming a very important feature of Dutch special education. When a child is transferred from a special to a regular school, he/she may receive assistance from the staff of the special school for as long as five years. The law specifies the number of hours of assistance to be provided to each pupil receiving peripatetic supervision.

Placement Procedures. Parents or teachers make an initial referral for assessment regarding the suitability of a special school placement. School boards then decide if the child may be admitted. The board is advised by a committee of experts who conduct an assessment. This committee generally consists of the head of the school, a doctor, a psychologist, and a social worker. After the assesment, the committee makes a recommendation to the school board, which then decides whether or not to admit the child. Parents may request a review of the decision.

Evaluation Procedures. Reassessment will occur within two years of placement. The reassessment indicates whether the child is placed appropriately, or whether a move to an ordinary school is called for. The review also focuses on the "school work plan", which "outlines the objectives, content and organization" of instruction, specifying, for example, the subject matter to be covered and the methods to be used to assess pupils' progress. This school work plan applies to the entire special school. It is supplemented by "activity plans" that specify how the school work plan is to be implemented with regard to individual pupils. The school work plans are prepared by the school staff, then submitted to an advisory council that includes parents. The school plan is then finalized by the school administration and presented to the education inspectorate for approval. Activity plans are "drawn up and, where necessary, modified in consultation with the parents of each child". Thus, the Netherlands is somewhat unique in specifying coordinated program planning and review at both the school and individual child levels.

Sweden

Placement Philosophy. Special education in Sweden is based on the principle of integration. The Swedish National Board of Education philosophy states that "compulsory school is to be adapted to the age and aptitudes of each individual pupil" (Emanuelsson, 1985, p. 3).

The Swedish documents are emphatic in their view that non-exceptional children, and society in general, benefit from the integration of youngsters with handicaps. Contact with handicapped children is seen as part of the educational experience of all other pupils.

Schools are responsible for developing solutions to "individual problems, problems of interaction, problems of school organization, and social problems" (p. 6). Providing for the needs of exceptional pupils is seen as one of the problems a school must solve.

Placement Policies. While integration and normalization are elements of law, some special schools for the developmentally challenged do exist. One of the documents acknowledges that Sweden has "a long way to go" in achieving the normalization its author advocates. Special schools are the major settings for continuing service delivery to developmentally challenged individuals aged 17 to 21 years. There is also some provision for special "therapy schools" for pupils with other exceptionalities. Enrolment in these must not be permanent. In compulsory schools, disabled pupils can be individually integrated into ordinary classes or placed in a special teaching group instead of remedial classes. Placements can therefore best be viewed as individual "action" programs. The National Swedish Board of Education indicates that pupils in difficulty require an action program based on:

- the definition of the problem
- a description of the goal
- a plan for the achievement of the goal

In 1988, a new compulsory school teacher education program, in which all teachers acquire some knowledge of special pedagogies, was introduced.

Placement Options. Most handicapped children in Sweden attend ordinary classes and schools. By altering current school teaching methods, small groups can be formed on a short-term basis. Courses of studies are adjusted to provide another possible modification within the framework of ordinary activities. Once every possible intervention at the classroom level has been attempted, and each has failed, participation in a special teaching group can be considered. Special teaching groups are organized at the school level. They appear to be organized in order to cluster together youngsters experiencing severe difficulty in meeting the academic and social demands of the school. In some cases, a pupil may receive the whole of his/her instruction in the special teaching groups, whereas others participate in the special group for some subjects only. The composition of these groups fluctuates with the turnover of pupils. The documents express some concern about the stigmatization of pupils in separate special teaching groups.

The aims of special day schools or therapy schools is to enable pupils to establish close contact with a limited number of adults, and activities are often conducted in association with the social welfare authorities. Every county in Sweden also has a psychiatric clinic for examining and treating children and young people, as well as treatment institutions and outpatient clinics.

Special schools for the developmentally challenged range from nursery schools to vocational schools. At the upper secondary school level, intellectually handicapped pupils attend vocational schools for the mentally retarded,* which are often located in the same premises as regular upper secondary schools.

Placement Procedures. Participation in the special teaching group is highly flexible and depends on a number of factors:

* Terminology used in original documents

- pupils in a group may require support for a number of different reasons;
- pupils must only attend the special teaching group for the length of time and the lessons for which they require special support; and
- pupils attending a special teaching group should belong to an ordinary class.

Placement in separate teaching groups is made by the public welfare conference acting in consultation with the pupil and her/his parents. This conference includes the pupil welfare staff (physician, nurse, social worker, school psychologist, guidance counsellor), the head teacher, and the class teacher. Sometimes the pupils and/or their parents attend as well. The pupil welfare conference is presented as a problem-solving unit, rather than as a placement committee, although placement in a special teaching group is one of the possible solutions to the problem of meeting the pupils' needs. Placement in a special teaching group requires consultation with both the pupils and their parents. (The Swedish and American documents are unique in their reference to pupil input into placement decisions.) In making these separate teaching group placement decisions, priority is given to pupils with the greatest difficulties.

Several classes in the school work together and pool their resources, including the efforts of teachers. This work unit often includes a remedial teacher, who can be involved in classroom work, or can take one or two pupils aside for remedial work.

Evaluation Procedures. Continuous evaluation of progress is a central part of the individual action program for pupils in difficulty. Several questions are asked as the pupil's program proceeds, such as:
- What experience is being gained? What are the goals in relation to work procedure?
- What use is being made of the experience gained? Is new knowledge being acquired?

On a more global level, county education committees in the principal localities each have a disabled services adviser, who coordinates and develops measures on behalf of disabled pupils, and makes plans for the "optimum use of available resources".

Switzerland

The responsibility for the organization of compulsory education in Switzerland lies with the 26 cantonal governments, each with its own educational legislation. All cantons provide supplementary school services such as psychological services and special education services. The federal government's role in special education is an advisory one.

Efforts at integration vary, depending on the peculiarities of the local school system. However, the documents received make it clear that self-contained special schools are the norm for pupils dealing with marked behaviour problems or more than mild developmental challenges; special classes in regular schools are intended for pupils with more minor difficulties.

Special classes in regular schools are available for children who are mildly emotionally disturbed* and who are slow learners.* These include special programs in which pupils take two years to complete first grade.

All placement procedures and evaluation are the responsibility of the cantons, and vary from one jurisdiction to the next. Specific information from cantons was not provided by Swiss federal authorities.

United States

Federal Public Law 94-142 mandated the child's right to a free, public education. This law encouraged the development of a philosophy of integration. Common elements are illustrated in Indiana's policies for placement of exceptional students, which was selected at random for detailed analysis.

* Terminology used in original documents

Placement Philosophy. A philosophy of placing students in the "least restrictive environment" implies placement to meet the child's "identified needs and approximates, as closely as possible, the educational placement of the non-handicapped child of comparable age and/or functional level" (Indiana State Board of Education, Rule S-1).

Placement Policies. Placement decisions are made by a Case Conference Committee composed of a representative of the school, other than the child's teacher, who is qualified to provide special education; the child's teacher; the parent of the child if the parent chooses; the child, if the child chooses, unless it can be demonstrated that the presence of the child is inappropriate; appropriate specialists; other individuals at the discretion of the parent or school.

A written case conference report includes: an individualized education program, a description of each evaluation procedure, test, record, or report used for the program, as well as any dissenting opinions; and a placement recommendation.

Placement Options. For pupils with minor developmental challenge, placement alternatives include:

- special consultation programs established to assist in meeting the needs of mentally handicapped* children whose special education needs can be met either in regular classrooms or in special classrooms for the mildly mentally handicapped;*
- instructional resource services, where children remain in the regular placement for the major part of the day except for scheduled tutorials or small-group instruction; and
- placement in special classes for the mildly mentally handicapped* for all or portions of the students' instructional program.

A number of alternative placements are suggested for seriously emotionally handicapped* students. These include:

- special consultation programs to assist in serving the needs of seriously emotionally handicapped children whose special education needs may be met in either regular classrooms or special classrooms. This consultation is related to the development and implementation of the child's individualized education program;
- instructional resource services, provided when children remain in their regular placement for the major portion of the day;
- assigment to special classes for the seriously emotionally handicapped* for all or portions of their instructional program.

The class sizes and caseload are limited to allow the teacher to meet the individual needs of both groups of exceptional children as specified by the individualized education plan.

Placement Procedures. The superintendent determines the available resources required to meet the needs of the child and produces a written notice that describes all evaluation procedures, tests, and records used as a basis for the determination. Placement procedures are stipulated by state Departments of Education.

Evaluation Procedures. Educational evaluation must be undertaken by a multidisciplinary team. It considers appropriate instructional task levels and reviews the child's achievement in basic social and academic skill areas. The evaluation procedures specified by all responding states were very specific. Objective indices of goal attainment are required for both academic and social objectives. The American procedures for the evaluation of pupil progress appear to be the most formal and detailed of any country in the sample.

---

* Terminology used in original documents

Summary of Responses from Other Countries

The documents received from other countries indicate considerable diversity. Placement philosophies range from integration to a wide range of special services, including special schools, which in some cases remain the primary setting for pupils with behavioural disorder and developmental challenge; this non-random sample was almost evenly split between the two approaches. Placement policies reflect such emphases as "normalization" of students (Denmark), "least restrictive environment" (Australia and United States), municipal responsibility (England, Denmark, Finland, Switzerland), demonstrated need of individual pupils (Germany, Sweden), and special federal funding (United States, Australia, Japan, the Netherlands, Germany, Sweden). Responsibility for carrying out policies rests primarily with the state authority (Australia, Germany, United States) or the municipal authority (Finland, United Kingdom, Japan, the Netherlands, Sweden, Switzerland). In many countries, there is a trend towards decentralization of decision making in recent years.

Despite this diversity, certain features seem almost universal. Placement decisions almost always involve a multidisciplinary team including competent professionals, in close contact with parents. With the exception of French-speaking Belgium, and possibly the U.S.A., there was little mandated specificity as to the exact data to be considered by these teams as a basis for their decisions. There is almost universal emphasis on continual monitoring of progress, including reassessment of the need for special placement, though few other countries seem to have mandated review procedures as formal as those of the United States.

The area of greatest divergence was the degree of centralization specified in the articulation of underlying philosophy. Several countries — for example, Denmark, Sweden, the U.K., and the U.S. — have adopted integration as a nationwide policy, though with considerable local autonomy as to how it is implemented. In contrast, special schools for pupils with the two exceptionalities studied here appear to remain the norm throughout the Netherlands, Germany, and Japan, though this is not as clearly articulated in national philosophy. Other countries, such as Australia and Switzerland, refrain from mandating a nationwide philosophy in order to provide for local autonomy. In these countries, the local authorities seem to opt for a wide range of placement alternatives.

Finally, the majority of other countries advocate programming based on individual pupil needs rather than categories of exceptionality. However, there were some important exceptions to this rule, such as Japan, the Netherlands, and French-speaking Belgium, whose documents suggest a clear commitment to categorization.

Other Canadian Provinces

A similar analysis of the documents provided by seven provinces and one territory in Canada was conducted to determine the placement philosophy, policies, program options, and evaluation procedures for behaviour-disordered and developmentally challenged pupils.

Alberta

School boards are responsible for developing relevant policies for all exceptional students in this province, within Ministry guidelines.

Placement Philosophy. Alberta Education adopts a philosophy of encouraging school jurisdictions to provide the "most enabling environment" for exceptional students.

Placement Policies. With the support of Alberta Education, school boards are responsible for the identification, assessment, and placement of exceptional students; the development and implementation of Individual Program Plans; and the evaluation of the individual progress of exceptional students. School boards are encouraged, whenever appropriate, to provide programs for exceptional students in regular school environments. Consultation with parents for placement is required, and procedures for hearing appeals are established.

Placement Options. Provisions for students "with challenging needs" vary from full-time integration to full-time separate provisions in self-contained settings.

Placement Procedures. The provincial government recommends a series of early identification procedures to school boards, including:

- informal identification where appropriate before grade 1
- diagnostic assessment on a one-to-one basis
- informal assessment/screening procedures
- specific, needs-oriented criteria for placement
- detailed student profiles, for use in placement decisions
- needs assessment survey before placement
- team approach to placement decisions
- multiple measures in intellectual assessment
- specification of teaching strategies
- clear entry and exit criteria, conveyed to staff
- central office review of all placements

School boards may determine that a student is "in need of a special education program. Once so identified, a student is entitled to have access to a special education program". The parent and, where appropriate, the student must be consulted. These decisions can be appealed. School boards are also responsible for the preparation of individual program plans. The Ministry of Education sees its role as advisory.

Evaluation Procedures. A variety of procedures are undertaken and student records are maintained. Recommendations relating to evaluation/review by Alberta school boards include proposals for:

- annual review of programs
- evaluation of behaviour/documentation for behavioural programs
- developing a system for evaluation
- consistent reporting for all schools
- case conference format to interpret test results
- monthly progress report to parents/discussing goals with parents/involving parents in total service plan
- weighted system for grades/criterion referenced testing/pre- and post-achievement tests (Alberta Education Response Centre, 1990, p. 8)

British Columbia

Placement Philosophy. The British Columbia Ministry of Education adopts a policy of integration for students with behaviour disorders. While there are specific documents pertaining to the identification of trainable mentally handicapped pupils (their term) and the level of service that must be provided to them, there is no discussion of integration in these documents.

Placement Policies. The British Columbia Ministry of Education considers the central issue to be not placement, but appropriate educational planning. Consistent with the philosophy of integration, policy specifies that a student should not be removed from the classroom unless all the facilities and services that can be delivered in the classroom have been made available and found to be insufficient. Written Individual Educational Plans (IEPs) must be developed for each student. Students, parents/guardians, school/district staff, and outside agencies are involved as appropriate. School districts are required to specify entrance and exit criteria for all special education programs.

Placement Options. School districts should offer a range of service options to behaviourally disordered students that include indirect consultative services, and may include opportunities for direct service by specialist personnel. These are educational programs designed to meet the special needs of students with severe behaviour disorders using resources obtained from a formal funding agreement between the Education, Health, Social Services and Housing ministries, and the Solicitor General. The documents explicitly state that "government ministries and agencies have accepted the responsibility to ensure that their policies and resources enhance a supportive environment for children's learning and well-being".

The possible learning environments include, but are not limited to:
- the classroom with additional support services
- the classroom with resource room contact
- a school-based program in a resource room or other specialized setting with some integration into regular classes
- a school-based specialized setting on a full-time basis
- a specialized setting outside the school
- short-term educational services in the student's home

Placement Procedures. There are a variety of referral and assessment procedures adopted by Rehabilitation Resources Advisory Committees composed of teachers, counsellors, child care workers, relevant community agency personnel, learning assistance teachers, school administrators, and district counsellors. The student and his or her parents may be full participants in any proceedings.

Evaluation Procedures. The Ministry specifies that every IEP should be reviewed on a regular basis. Evaluation occurs at designated times during the year. The IEP form is also a tracking tool used to manage the student's program. In addition to this evaluation procedure for individual pupils' programs, British Columbia mandates evaluation of programs funded under interministerial agreement; these evaluation procedures are specified in the protocols establishing each interministerial program.

Manitoba

Placement Philosophy. Manitoba favours a philosophy of placing all special needs students in the most "enabling" environment.

Placement Policies. Educational placement of students is to be based on a systematic assessment of specific individual needs rather than by category of learning problems. Placement and evaluation procedures are not indicated in the documents reviewed.

Placement Options. Developmentally challenged students, at the elementary level, are at least partially integrated into regular classrooms with special supports. At the secondary level, students receive programming in special-class settings with partial integration where possible.

Students with severe behaviour disorders are provided program options ranging from small special-class placement to regular-class placement with teacher assistant support. Some pupils with extreme behavioural disorders attend special education programs in institutional treatment settings.

New Brunswick

Bill 85 mandates integration of exceptional students. School districts are working towards disbanding special classes and providing resource room and/or collaborative consultative models of service. The documents do not provide detail as to the extent to which the new approach, now five years old, has been implemented.

Placement Philosophy. New Brunswick has adopted a philosophy of integration into the regular classrooms. Students with intellectual, developmental, and behavioural disabilities are referred to as exceptional students, and not categorized by type of disability.

Placement Policies. Bill 85 emphasizes individual programming and requires that school boards integrate exceptional pupils in regular classrooms with non-exceptional pupils unless such placement proves detrimental to the needs of the child or other children. The legislation requires that a case must be made to remove a child from a regular class, rather than requiring a case to be made to keep the child there (New Brunswick Department of Education, 1988).

Placement Options. A range of special services, supports, and programs are required. Some examples are: curriculum modifications, various evaluation procedures, adapted teaching methods, alternative assignments and materials, room programs, adjusted timetables, physical modifications to classrooms and/or buildings. Support may be provided by the principal as educational leader, and other professionals along with parent and community volunteers. Support is also provided to regular classroom teachers through release time for planning with parents and other professionals, classroom inservice training, and visits to exemplary practice sites.

Placement Procedures. Exceptional students are placed in regular classrooms automatically. A special case must be made for removal from the regular classroom. Evaluation procedures are not specified in the documents received, nor are criteria for the adjudication of these special cases.

Newfoundland and Labrador

Placement Philosophy. The Department of Education espouses a philosophy based on providing the most "enhancing" environment for students with special needs. The documents indicate that every effort should be made to move special education students to an integrated environment whenever possible. The view is that most students would begin their formal eduction in regular classroom settings with special help. Students should be "moved to specialized and limited settings only when this is required by their instructional program" (Government of Newfoundland and Labrador, 1979, Guidelines 2. A. 4.).

Placement Policies. A general policy relegates responsibility to the 31 school districts. School districts are expected to provide a wide range of services and to avoid using labels except when applying for funds or accounting for expenditures. School districts must establish planning teams at the school level responsible for programming and evaluation.

Placement Options. A wide range of services based on the "cascade" model include: diverse regular educational environments, diverse educational environments with special education supports; specialized educational environments, such as a special education class but with students integrated into the regular program for subjects and activities from which the students will benefit; and limited self-contained educational environments. In some cases exceptional students receive educational services in institutions (e.g., hospitals, correctional centres).

Placement Procedures. Screening and identification is done by classroom teacher in consultation with school personnel. Evaluation information is compiled by the school program planning team. While the documents did not specify procedures for identification, placement, or placement review, the respondent indicated that new guidelines were in preparation. Existing procedures appear to vary considerably among school boards.

Evaluation Procedures. Special education teachers, with the support of the program planning team, must review and evaluate student placement and progress.

Northwest Territories

The Northwest Territories Department of Education has adopted the principle of the least restrictive environment for placement of exceptional students. Categorical labels are not used. Special needs students are those who, following assessment, are considered by an Individual Education Program team to require additional support.

Placement Philosophy. The guiding philosophy espouses the principle that for special needs students an Individual Education Program should be implemented in the least restrictive environment, with age-appropriate peers. Government resources should be channelled to support community-based non-institutional programs.

Placement Policies. It is not the policy of the Department of Education to establish classes for special needs students.

Placement Options. Classroom teachers are given the primary responsibility for students, including those with special needs. Levels of support include a full-time Special Needs Assistant, a part-time Special Needs Assistant, and small group support.

Placement Procedures. The documents indicated that students should be placed with their age-appropriate peer group whenever possible, including those receiving instruction in special hospital settings. Modifications to the classroom environment and the classroom program should occur. Support for the classroom teacher is seen as essential.

Evaluation Procedures. Ongoing evaluation practices and procedures intended to measure the student's performance are recommended.

Prince Edward Island

In this province, developmentally challenged children are placed in regular classes with teacher assistants. P.E.I. has a few special classes for these children located in regular schools. Students in these special classes are withdrawn for activities with regular classes when possible. Emotionally/behaviourally disordered students at the elementary level are assigned a one-on-one teacher assistant who works with them in class or withdraws them for teaching when needed. Adolescents receive services in the "Adolescent Unit", which is a treatment centre located on the campus of the psychiatric hospital.

Saskatchewan

Placement Philosophy. Saskatchewan education philosophy expects that "Exceptional pupils should experience education in settings that allow them to achieve their specified learning goals in the most appropriate environment" (Saskatchewan Education, 1989, p. 3).

Placement Policies. The local board of education is responsible for determining placement of pupils. Placement of pupils in other than the ordinary program of the school must be done with the knowledge of, and in consultation with, parents or guardians. In addition, Saskatchewan Education requires that school boards develop a comprehensive master plan for serving exceptional pupils at both the school district and individual school levels.

Guiding principles for special education specify that "placement decisions should be the result of planning and consultative process that involves parents or guardians, educators, and support personnel" (p. 11). Considerations in making placement decisions should include the following:

- placement should occur as close to home as possible;
- maximum opportunities should be provided for interaction between disabled and non-disabled pupils; and
- support services should be available as an integral part of the special education program.

In a somewhat unique provision, placement of the "socially emotionally (behaviourally) disabled" requires that "an evaluation of the school setting should establish that inappropriate school expectations are not the cause or a contributing factor".

Placement Options. Program modifications for the developmentally challenged may include adapted or alternative curricula, support staff in the classroom, or a variety of locally determined provisions. For the socially, emotionally, or behaviourally disabled, modifications may include:

- a teacher assistant for behavioural management
- a special class
- a special school

Placement Procedures. Mental health and/or community health teams "may suggest appropriate interventions in the school or other settings and make placement decisions in consultation with the school teams".

Evaluation Procedures. Special education program provisions for pupils identified as high cost must be reviewed at least annually by the responsible school division, but no specific formal review or evaluation of individual programs is required.

Summary of Responses from Other Canadian Provinces

From the provincial documents received, it appeared that there were common features and trends in the education of behaviour-disordered and developmentally challenged students in Canada. There is a clear trend towards the formal recognition of special education programs as an integral part of the total school program. Common features include: an ongoing search for an acceptable philosophy for the education of special needs students; development of ways to implement individualized services for students in need; reflection upon the names and purposes of programs to avoid unnecessary labelling; and establishment of a master plan that includes evaluation for delivery of services by school districts. The documents indicate a growing emphasis on integration across the country.

Responses from Ontario School Boards

An analysis of the Ontario school board policy documents was conducted to determine trends concerning the placement philosophies, policies, options, and procedures, as well as the evaluation procedures, for students with behavioural disorders and developmentally challenged students. Responses were received from a total of 123 Ontario school boards.

Seven of these were eliminated after an initial scan because they were too brief and did not enable an understanding of the board's philosophies, procedures, and policies. One-fourth of the remaining boards were selected randomly for in-depth document review. (This procedure is somewhat different from the stratified sampling procedure used for on-site data collection [See Section 2].) This analysis was based on documents provided by a random sample of 29 Ontario school boards from June to September 1990. Each set of documents was reviewed and a summary made of the placement philosophy, policies, procedures, and evaluation provisions. A frequency count was made to determine the numbers of school boards that had provided documents relevant to the five research questions enumerated at the beginning of this section. The documents were then analyzed to identify the common elements and the range of approaches used by the boards to address each of the five research questions.

As is the case in many school and ministry documents, "philosophy" and "policy" were sometimes closely related terms in the documents analyzed. In some cases, board documents used the terms interchangeably. In order to clarify this distinction, our analysis was guided by conceptual distinctions between philosophy and policy commonly outlined in policy analysis literature. Accordingly, "philosophy" was distinguished as guiding principles, often expressed as an initial statement of "placement philosophy" in board documents. Board policies were distinguished as allocative determinations implied in sets of proposed actions outlined in those documents.

Placement Philosophy

As depicted in Figure 1.1, over half of the 29 boards that provided policy documents regarding the placement of developmentally challenged and behaviour-disordered pupils did not include a clearly articulated placement philosophy for these exceptional children that could be discerned by our research staff. One school board indicated a philosophy for students with behaviour disorders only. In this case, the board expressed the belief that pupils with behavioural exceptionalities should be placed in as normal a school setting as possible, and should be placed in regular classrooms with the necessary support provided for both the pupil and the teacher. Three of the 29 boards provided documents indicating placement philosophies for the developmentally challenged only. One of these specifically indicated a philosophy of placing the developmentally challenged in classes with same-age peers as much as possible. All three boards adopted what they described as an "integrative philosophy".

Placement philosophies applying to all exceptionalities were described by 10 school boards. Several of these referred to the need for a range of services, including both integrated and segregated settings. Various terms were used by boards to characterize the placement philosophy advocating a range of services, including "enabling", "maximizing", and "optimal". Two boards specifically advocated providing educational services for both exceptionalities in as "normal a setting" as possible. Both of these boards defined a normal setting as the student's "home school". One of the 29 Ontario school boards developed a comprehensive philosophical statement to guide special education services termed "mainstreaming". Three school boards cited Ontario Regulation 544/81 as their placement philosophy, referring, for example, to the requirements for forming an Identification, Placement, and Review Committee (IPRC). Figure 1.2 depicts a clustering of the documents by central philosophical concept.

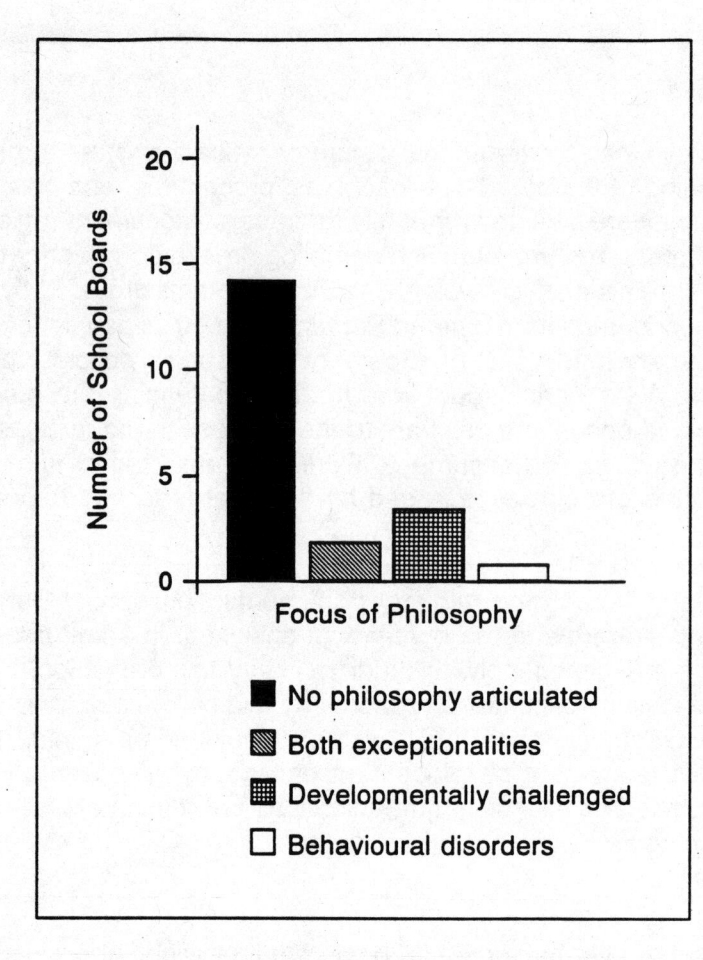

Figure 1.1 Focus of Placement Philosophy – Ontario Sample

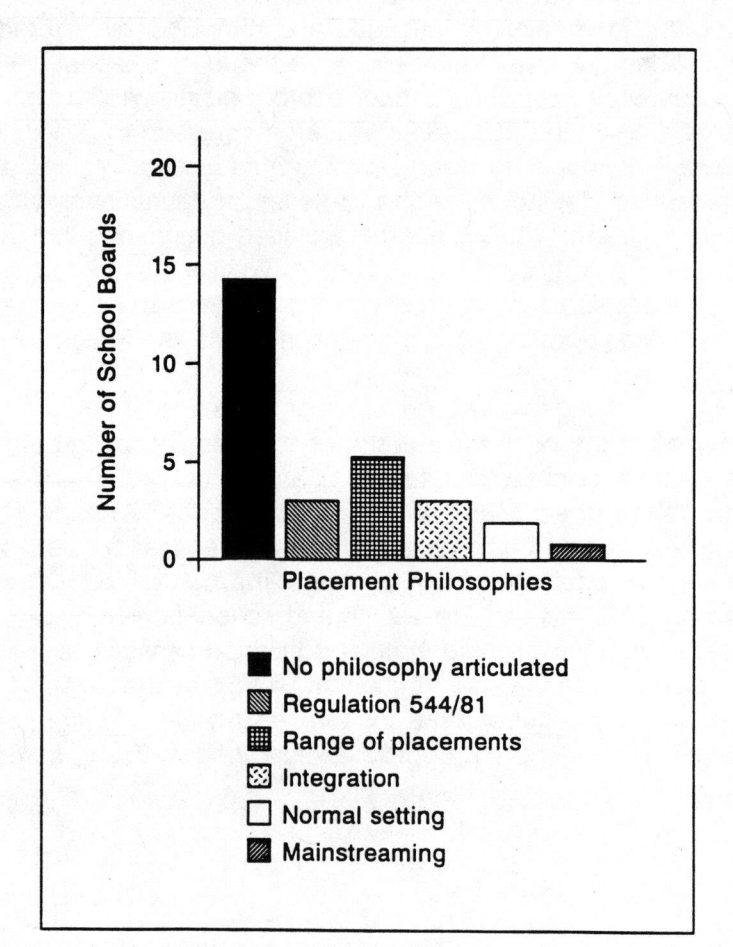

- ■ No philosophy articulated
- ▨ Both exceptionalities
- ▦ Developmentally challenged
- □ Behavioural disorders

Figure 1.2 Clusters of Placement Philosophies – Ontario Sample

- ■ No philosophy articulated
- ▨ Regulation 544/81
- ▦ Range of placements
- ▧ Integration
- □ Normal setting
- ▨ Mainstreaming

Placement Policies

Analysis of policy documents provided by this sample of 29 school boards revealed a range of policy development and policy focus. As shown in Figure 1.3, many boards did not indicate any specific placement policies (n = 13). Others indicated that Regulation 544/81 was their placement philosophy (n = 5); some of these simply restated the procedures specified in the regulation, while others elaborated on them somewhat. Two boards provided a general policy for placement of special students; the remaining boards had specific policies regarding either or both of the exceptionalities under study.

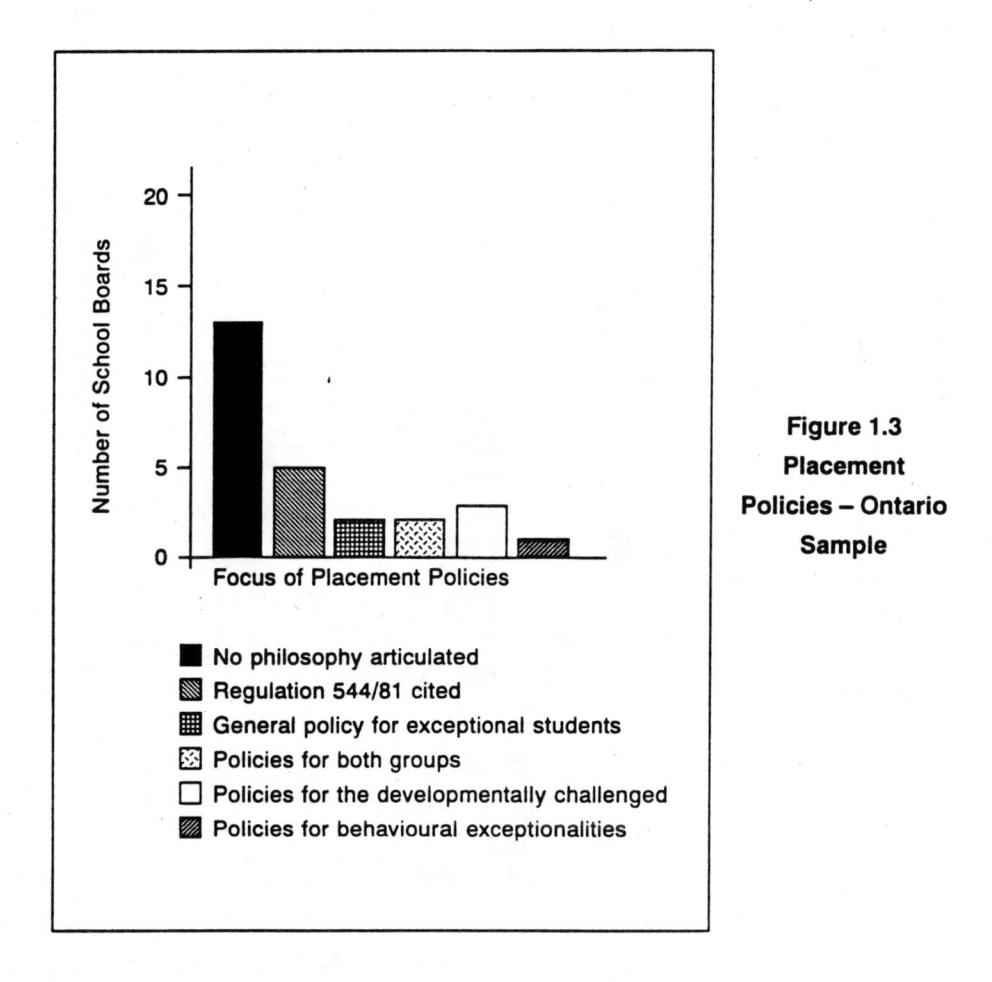

Figure 1.3 Placement Policies – Ontario Sample

Ten of the 29 boards had adopted placement policies that went beyond mandated requirements. One of these articulated its own established placement policies, based on its philosophy of mainstreaming, which applied to all students with special needs. This board had a clear and consistent set of policies and procedures regarding the placement of all students with special needs. This board also established a seven-stage model of service delivery for behavioural exceptionality, based on the concepts of prevention, mainstreaming, and individualization of program. The majority of the remaining nine boards articulated policies that specified placing pupils in the least restrictive environment possible, or integrated with regular pupils as far as possible. A few others emphasized the range of settings and specified that pupils should be placed in the setting most suited to their needs.

Evaluation Procedures

The provisions for evaluation are depicted in Figure 1.4. Most of the boards (n = 16) in this sample did not indicate any specific evaluation procedures for the progress of behaviour-disordered or developmentally challenged pupils, or for services offered this population. Another eight boards simply reiterated the provisions outlined in Regulation 544/81. A few boards elaborated slightly on these provisions. In sharp contrast, one board had prepared a detailed set of guidelines for evaluation. These guidelines specified the judicious use of observational techniques, with support materials to be developed to illustrate these techniques to teachers. It directed that existing methods of evaluation be examined for racial, gender, and class bias, and that explicit directions be provided regarding the use and misuse of standardized tests. It also indicated that alternative methods of assessment should be used with pupils new to the country who do not understand English.

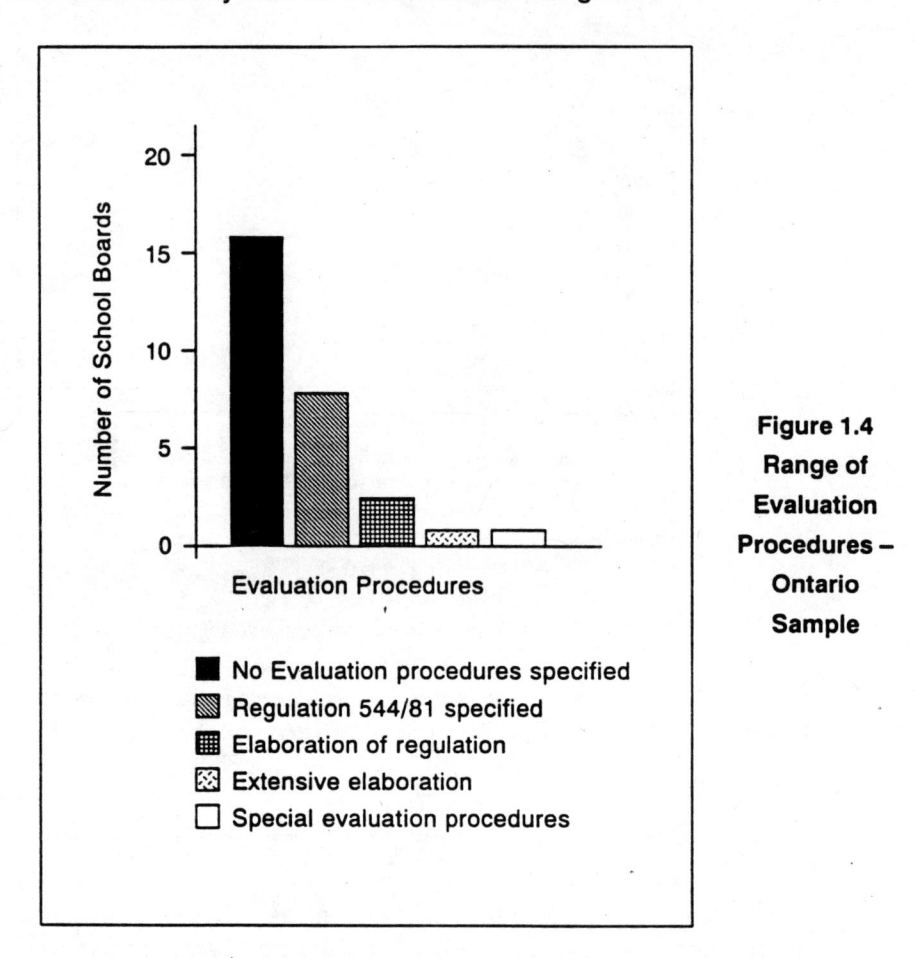

Figure 1.4 Range of Evaluation Procedures – Ontario Sample

Comparison of Documents from Ontario and Those from Other Jurisdictions

The scope of this review is limited to the analysis of the documents received. The Ontario-based research team has no way of determining how well the philosophies and procedures detailed therein are implemented at the "grass roots" level, nor how teachers, parents, administrators, and pupils outside Ontario feel about them; therefore, the following observations are presented with some caution.

Few of the themes discussed in the policy and procedures documents received from other countries and provinces will be unfamiliar to the reader who is familiar with the Ontario education scene. Nevertheless, this review has made it possible to situate Ontario within the configuration of policies and procedures that have been established across Canada and in other countries with similar resources. As indicated above, many countries and provinces have established a firm central guiding policy to which individual localities and schools must conform. This central policy is often one of integration or mainstreaming. Ontario appears to be among the other group of jurisdictions, which allow greater flexibility for development of placement philosophy at the local level, though the Ministry has stated that integrated options should be available. Despite this flexibility, only a minority of school boards appear to have articulated a conclusive position regarding the placement of the two groups of exceptional children studied here.

Jurisdictions vary in their emphasis on categorization of exceptionalities, with some insisting on a non-categorical approach. Ontario is one of the locations in which categories are a fundamental feature of legislation and program philosophy.

The procedures mandated in Ontario for the placement of exceptional children and review of their progress appear to typify modal practice in most of the jurisdictions reviewed, though the Ontario procedures are probably more formal than those of most other provinces. In common with most other jurisdictions, evaluation is prescribed at the level of the individual pupil program, including continuous assessment of the educational objectives for individual pupils. The most specific and standard procedures for the review of individual pupil progress appear to emanate from the United States, where they have accompanied the implementation of federal laws regarding the education of exceptional learners. Relatively few jurisdictions mandate program evaluation at the level of the program, class, unit, school, treatment setting, or, indeed, province or country.

References

Alberta Education Response Centre. (!990). **Summary of evaluation reports: Common features and trends in special education**. Edmonton, ALB: Author.

Danish Ministry of Education. (1986), **Handicapped students in the Danish educational system**. Copenhagen, Denmark: Author.

Emanuelsson, Ingemar. (1985). **Integration of handicapped pupils in Sweden: Concepts, research experience, present practices** (Reports No. S-106-42). Stockholm, Sweden: National Swedish Board of Education.

Government of Newfoundland and Labrador. (1979). **Special education policy manual**. St. John's, NFLD: Author.

New Brunswick Department of Education. (1988). **Working guidelines on integration**. Fredericton, NB: Author.

Saskatchewan Education. (1989). **Special education policy manual**. Regina, SASK: Author.

Western Australia Ministry of Education (1984). **Changes to services for children in need of educational support**.

SECTION 2

COMPARISON ACROSS JURISDICTIONS OF DEFINITIONS AND PREVALENCE RATES

ABSTRACT

This section is also based on responses to the survey reported in Section 1. It compares the jurisdictions in terms of the number of pupils identified as behaviour disordered and developmentally challenged. The proportion of these pupils placed in various special education settings by different school boards in Ontario is also compared.

Sections 1, 4, and 6 of this report involve comparisons across jurisdictions of policies and provisions for pupils identified as having either or both of the exceptionalities studied by this research team, namely, behaviour disorder and moderate developmental challenge. Such comparisons must be made with caution, for many reasons. Foremost among the obstacles in comparing perceptions across jurisdictions is that the informants may not be referring to the same group of children. The purpose of this section is to explore these differences in the concepts and prevalence rates of the two disorders.

The prevalence of both behaviour disorder and developmental challenge is influenced by many factors, including social and economic conditions. Communities may also differ in their tolerance of atypical behaviour and in the proportion of youngsters they perceive as atypical (this applies more specifically to the behaviour-disordered group). Some authorities in special education have also pointed out that prevalence rates are affected by political and economic considerations. Identification may be higher where the referral source perceives identification as a vehicle for access to services for the child, school, or community in question (Magliocca and Stephens,1980). On the other hand, identification may be reduced if the referral source perceives it as leading to stigma, or where resources are insufficient to effect program changes consistent with the disorder identified.

Method

Questionnaires asking for details and documentation regarding the definition of developmentally challenged and behaviour-disordered students, as well as placements and personnel services available to students of the two exceptionalities, were sent to all school boards in Ontario, all Ministries of Education in Canada, all U.S. state Departments of Education, and the embassies or high commissions of other major Western countries and Japan. The purpose of the questionnaire was: (1) to obtain details regarding the definition of developmentally challenged and behaviour-disorderd students in use in the different regions and countries; and (2) to explore the services, as they vary across regions, that are available to the students identified as belonging to the two exceptionalities. No conjectures will be offered to explain degrees of difference (variations) across the locations. The intent here is to depict similarities and differences among the various jurisdictions.

Questionnaires were sent to the following:

- all 176 school boards in Ontario, of which 123 replied;
- all Ministries of Education in Canada, of which 9/12 replied;
- all states of the United States of America, of which 25 replied;
- Sweden, Denmark, Finland, the Netherlands, Belgium, Germany, Switzerland, France, England, Ireland, South Africa, Australia, and Japan, of which all but France replied.

The responses from several jurisdictions (e.g., Australia) indicated that, consistent with their non-categorical approach, pupils are not formally identified and therefore statistics are not available. These comparisons are based on 14 American states and 9 other countries that provided usable data.

Results

Ontario Sample

Of the 123 replies from the Boards of Education in Ontario, 107 responses yielded the information that was used in this survey. These boards represented a total enrolment of 1,602,669 students. The responding boards were grouped by region and support (either public or separate) in Table 2.1.

The following is a summary of responses by survey question:

Definitions

Does your Board have established policies for identification, placement, and/or review regarding the two exceptionalities?

Seventy percent of the boards indicated that they had policies. Section 1 was a detailed report of a sub-sample of these.

Variations in Placement

How many children of these two exceptionalities are served in the different kinds of delivery systems?

The proportion of students of each of the two exceptionalities served by three types of delivery systems, viz., regular classroom, special classroom, and special schools, for each district and by support, are shown in Figures 2.1 to 2.4

All Responding Public Boards (September Reports, 1987)		
District	**Number of Boards**	**Total Student Enrolment**
Central	19	513 345
Eastern	10	164 381
Mid-Northern	7	38 247
North-Eastern	9	38 100
North-Western	8	29 460
Western	8	135 926
Metro-Toronto	5	234 973

All Responding Separate Boards (September Reports, 1987)		
District	**Number of Boards**	**Total Student Enrolment**
Central	13	195 534
Eastern	6	70 421
Mid-Northern	4	29 851
North-Eastern	6	11 108
North-Western	6	11 543
Western	5	25 105
Metro-Separate	1	104 675

Table 2.1   Total Student Enrolment in Responding Boards

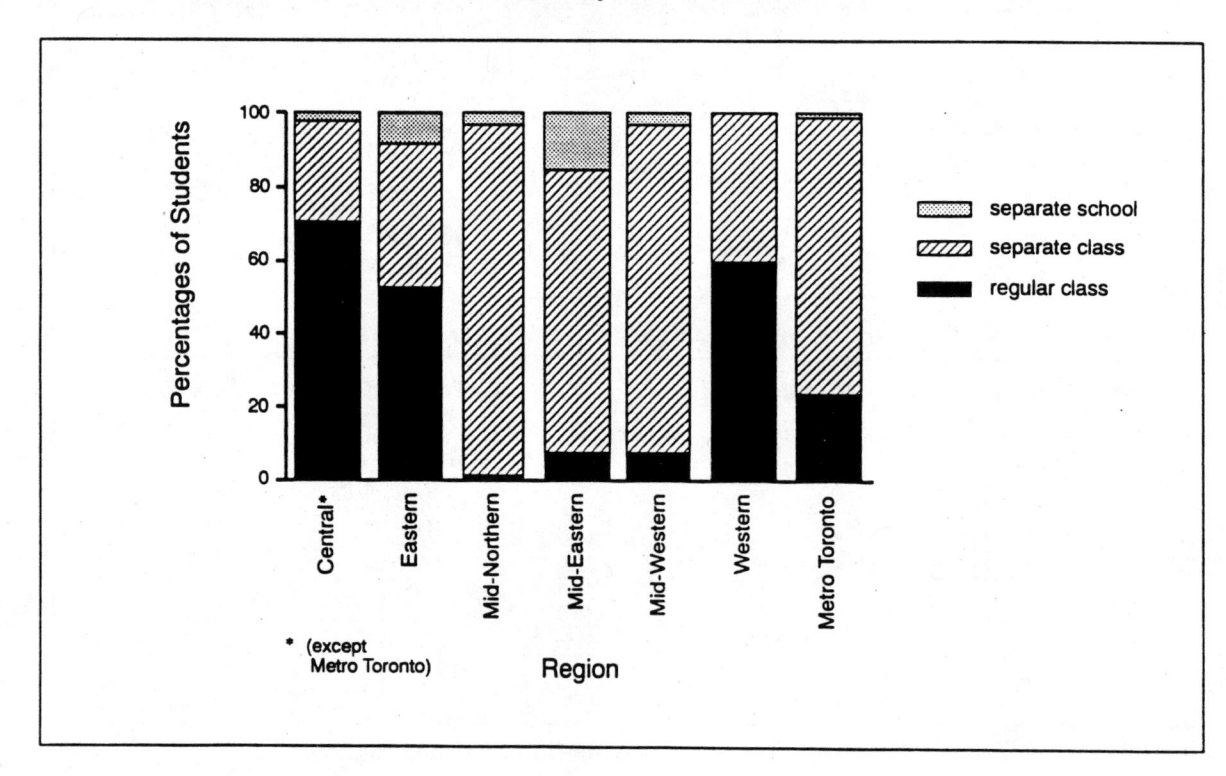

Figure 2.1
Distribution of Developmentally Challenged Pupils by Placement Setting:
Ontario Public Boards

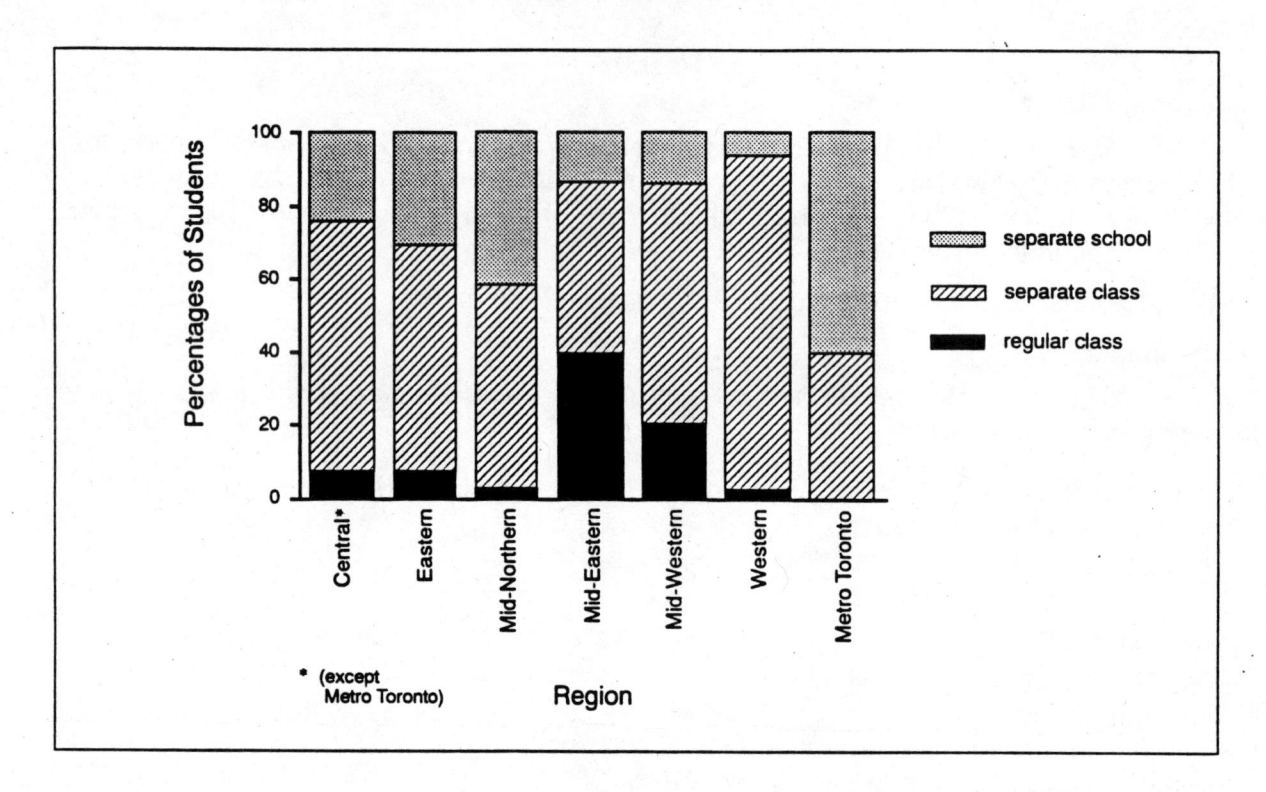

Figure 2.2
Distribution of Developmentally Challenged Pupils by Placement Setting:
Ontario Separate Boards

**Figure 2.3
Distribution of Behaviour-Disordered Pupils by Placement Setting:
Ontario Public Boards**

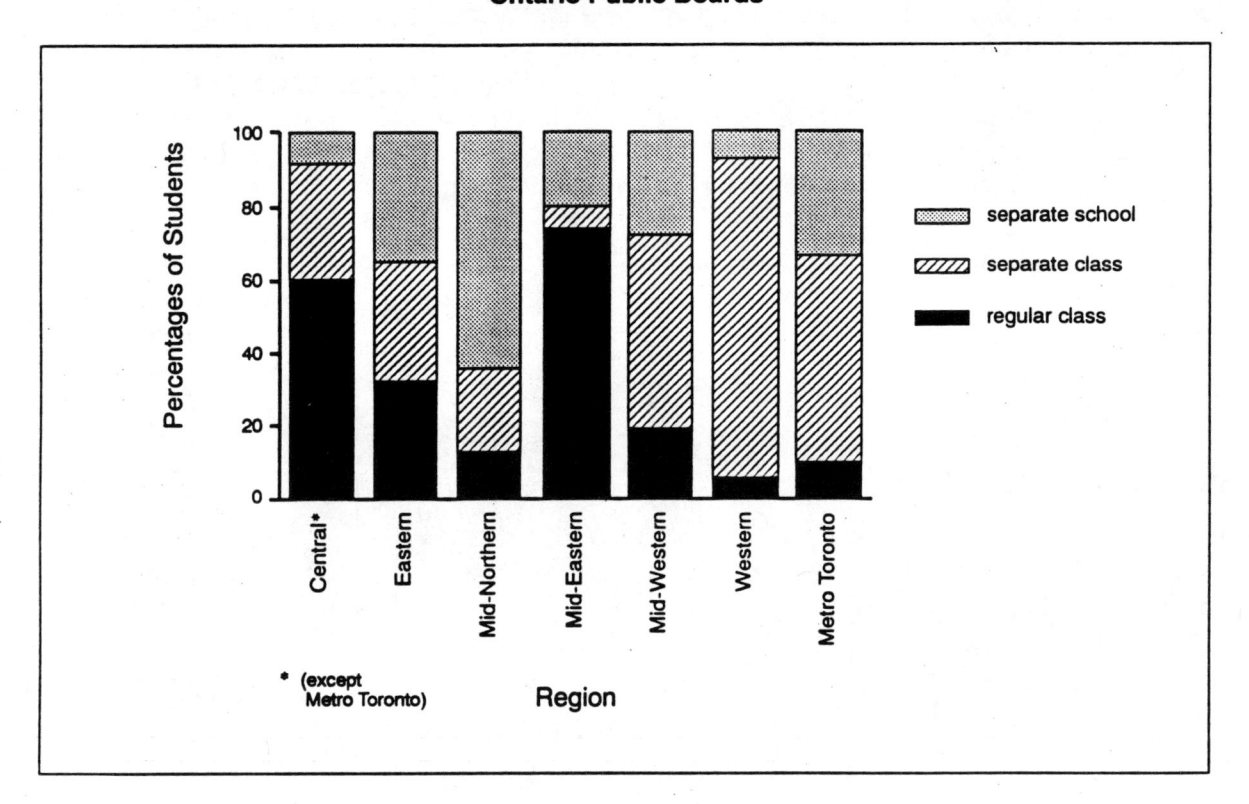

**Figure 2.4
Distribution of Behaviour-Disordered Pupils by Placement Setting:
Ontario Separate Boards**

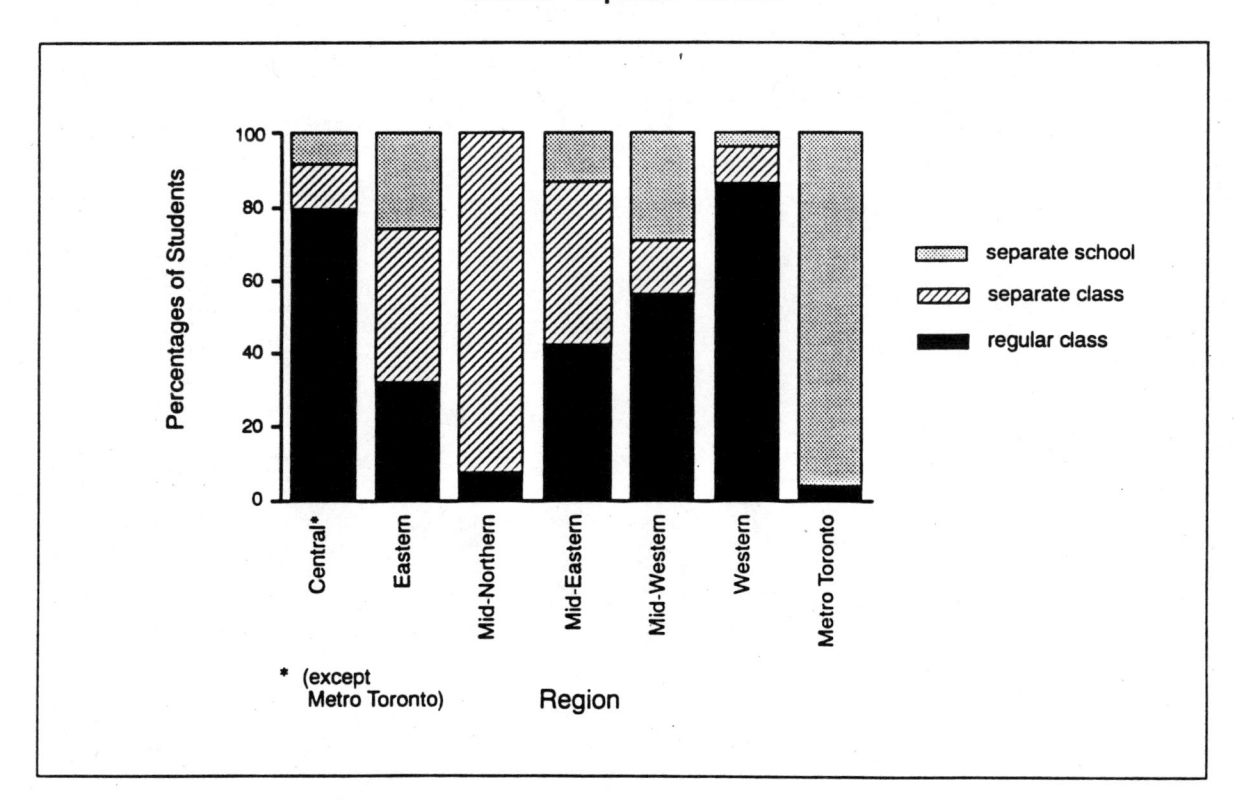

Prevalence Rates

Prevalence rates for each of the two disorders were calculated, by dividing the number of identified pupils by the total board enrolment. The prevalence of the developmentally challenged enrolment figures for the Metropolitan Toronto public schools was calculated by dividing the Metro Toronto board enrolment of developmentally challenged students by the total enrolments of all public school boards within Metropolitan Toronto. The results are depicted graphically in Figures 2.5 to 2.9, along with comparable figures from other countries. Median are reported in order to minimize the weight of any idiosyncratic extreme responses.

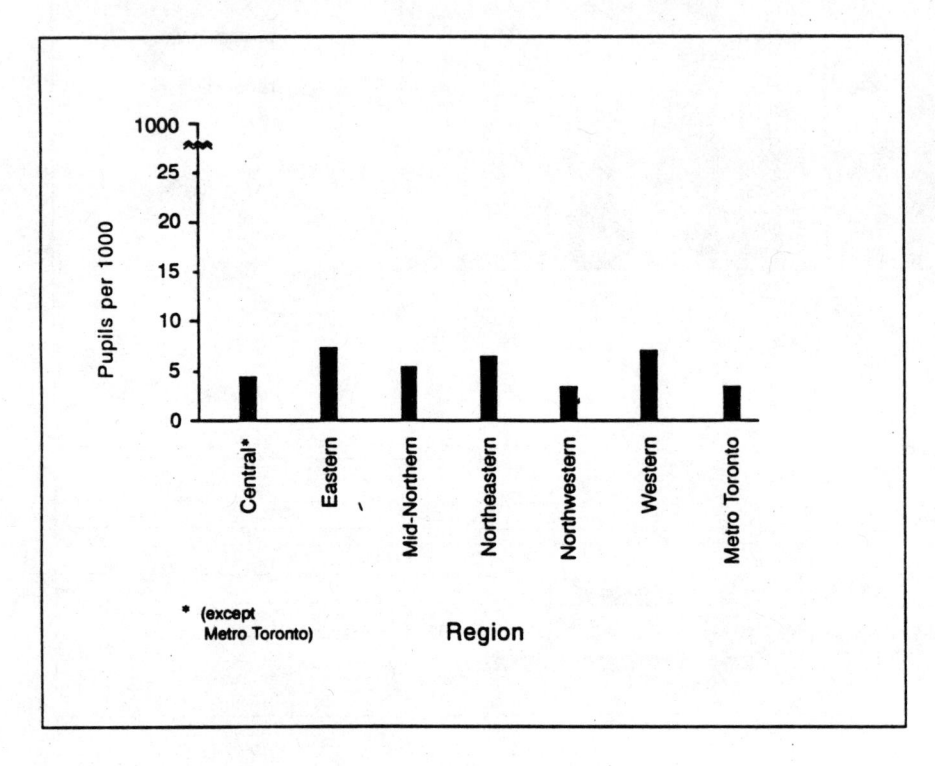

Figure 2.5A Ontario Public Boards: Developmentally Challenged Median Prevalence According to Survey Responses

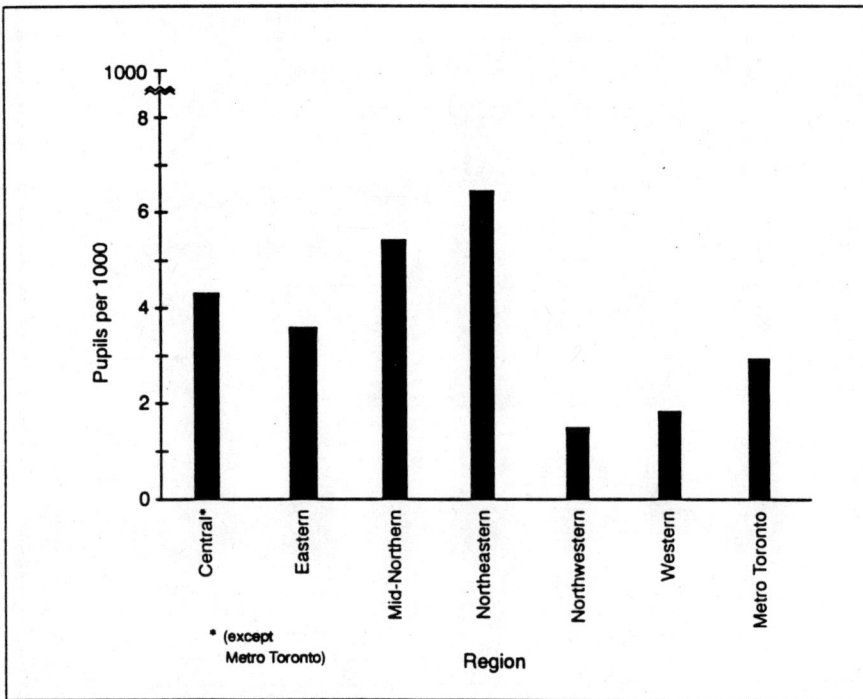

Figure 2.5B Ontario Separate Boards: Developmentally Challenged Median Prevalence According to Survey Responses

**Figure 2.6A
Ontario Public Boards: Behaviour-Disordered Median Prevalence
According to Survey Responses**

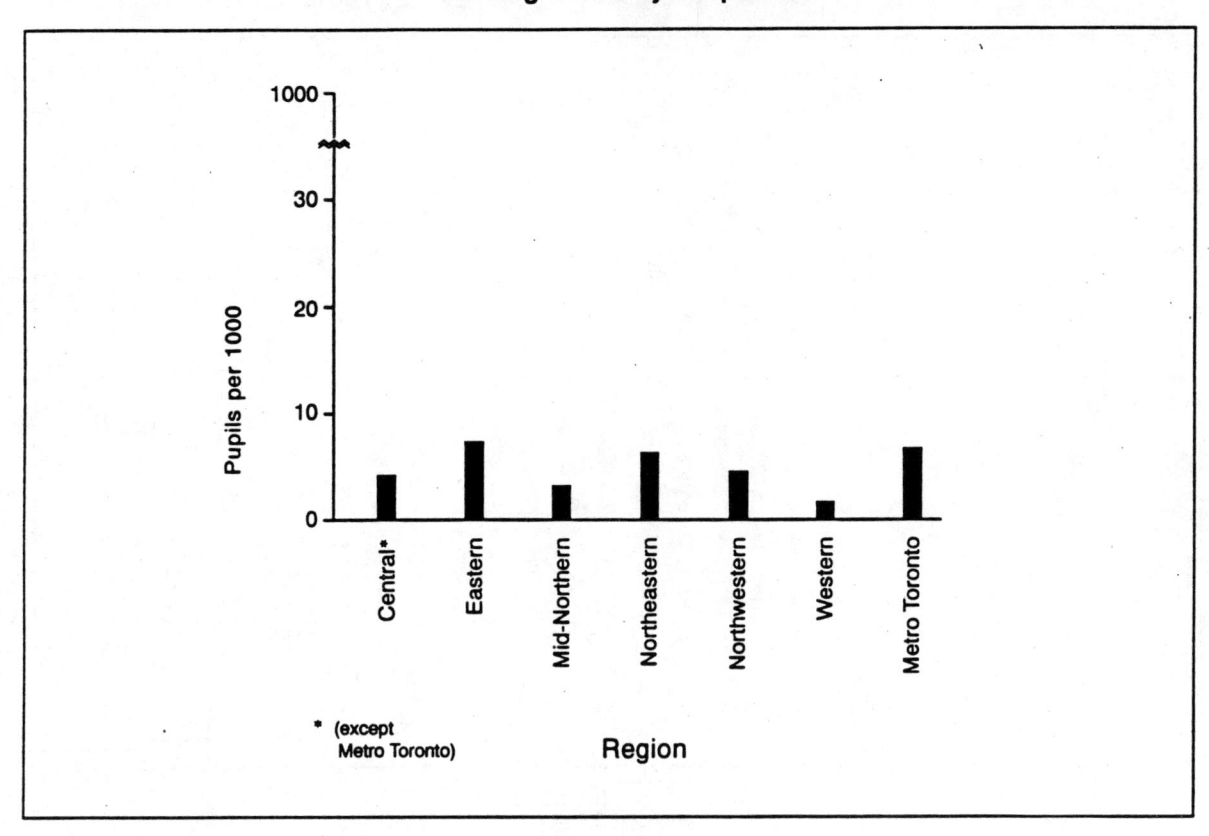

**Figure 2.6B
Ontario Separate Boards: Behaviour-Disordered Median Prevalence
According to Survey Responses**

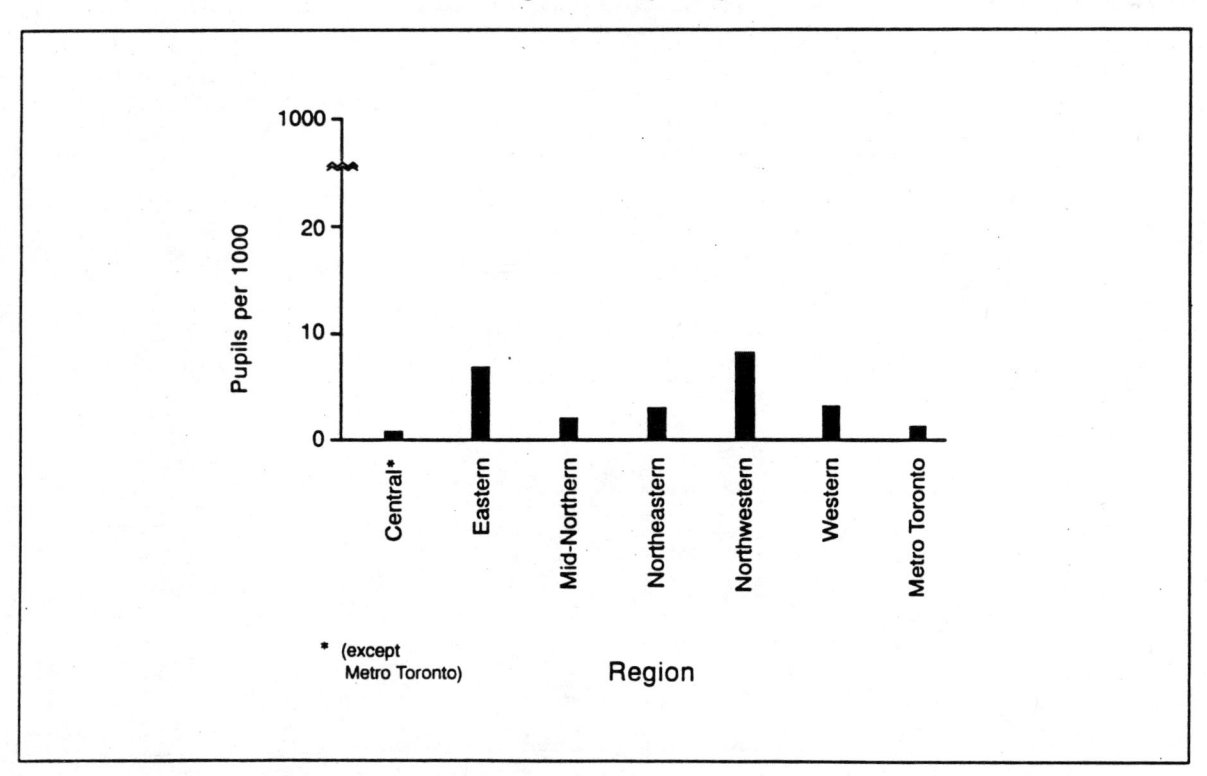

Figure 2.7A
**All Ontario Boards: Behaviour-Disordered Median Prevalence
According to Survey Responses**

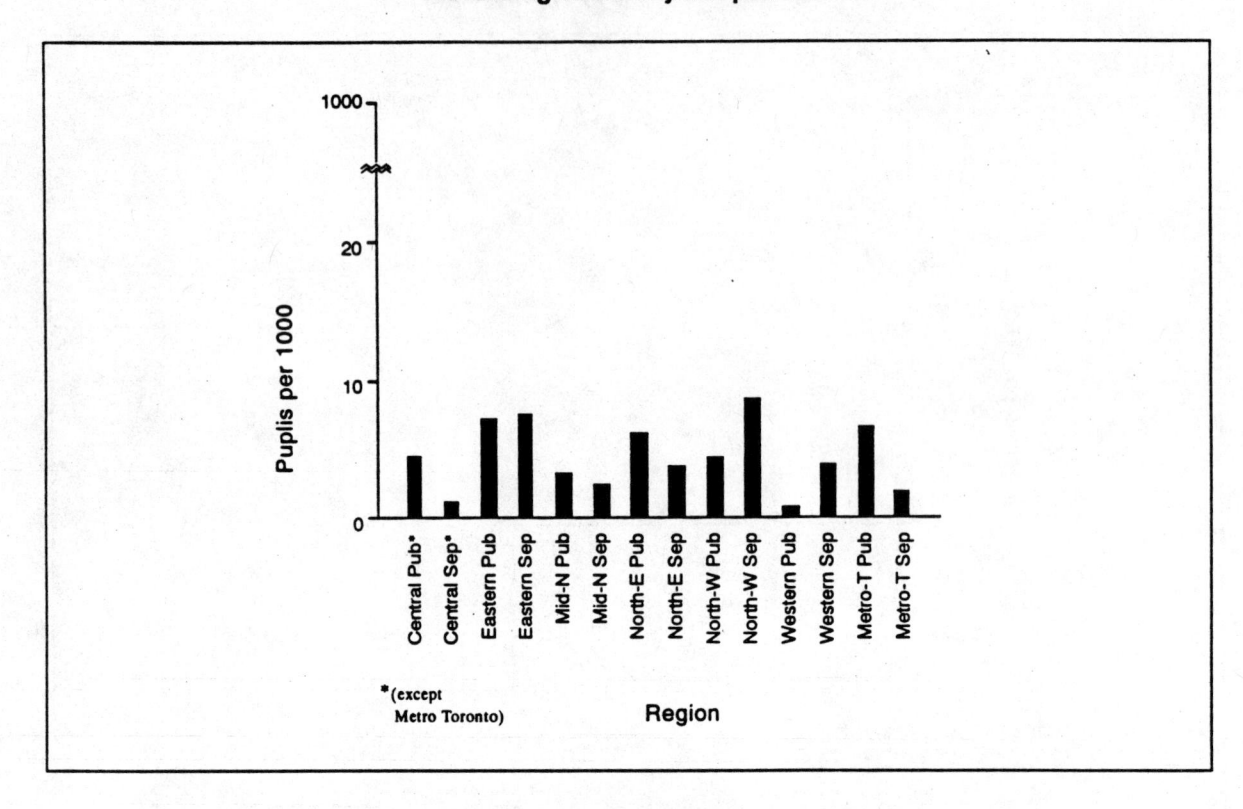

Figure 2.7B
**All Ontario Boards: Developmentally Challenged Median Prevalence
According to Survey Responses**

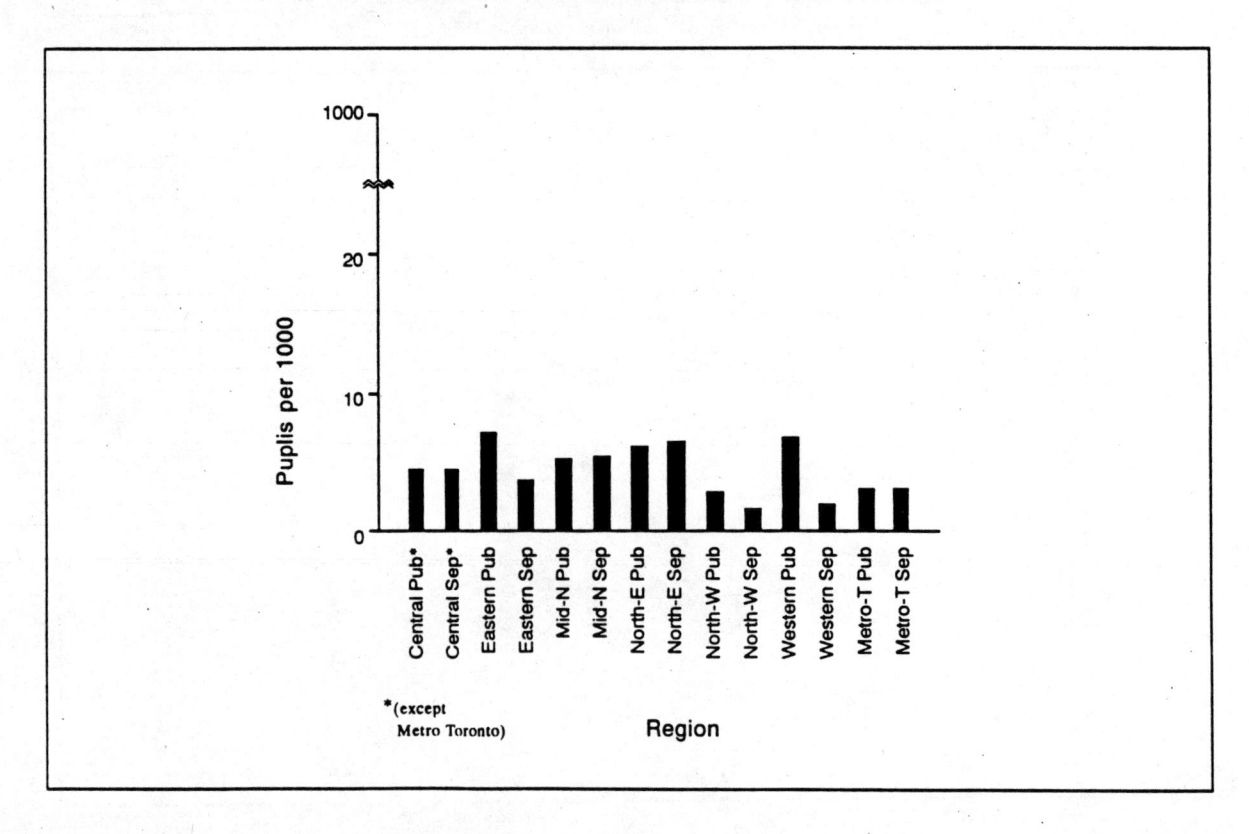

Figure 2.8
Ontario, United States, Europe, Japan: Prevalence of Developmentally Challenged

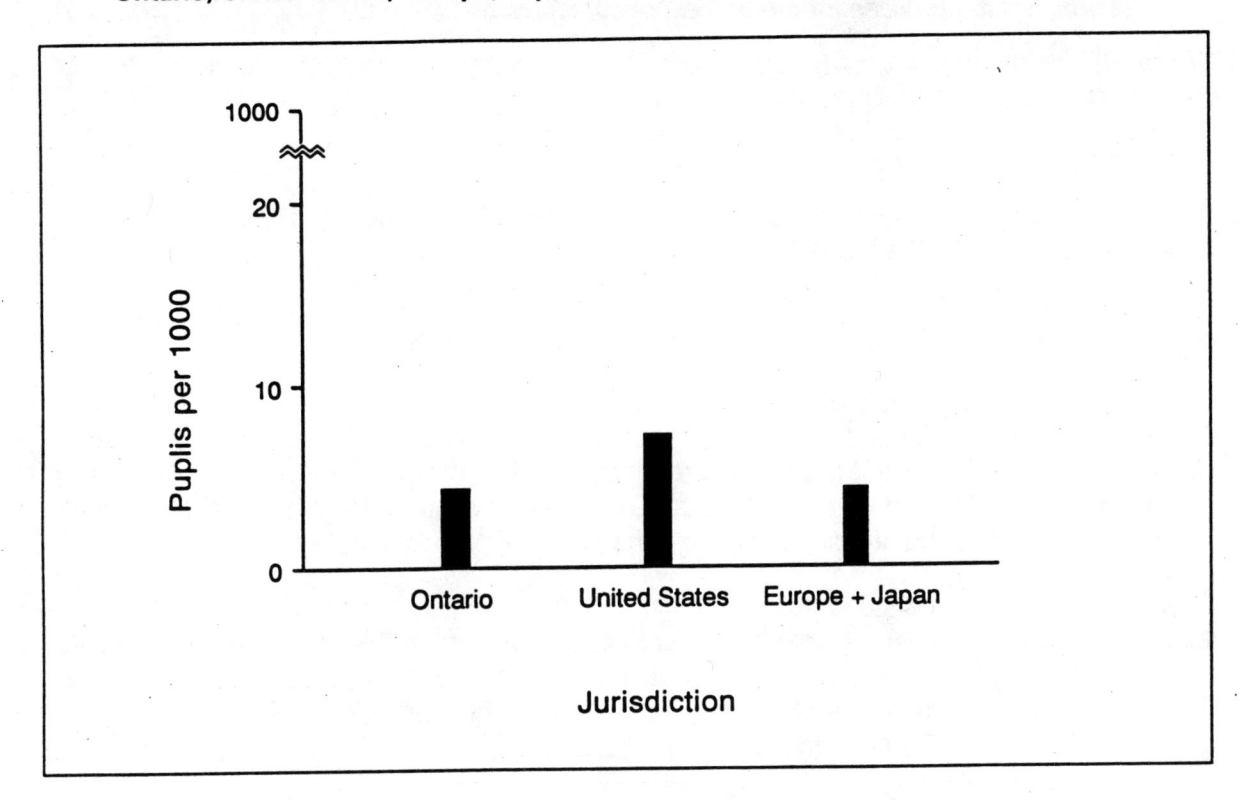

Figure 2.9
Ontario, United States, Europe, Japan: Prevalence of Behaviour Disordered

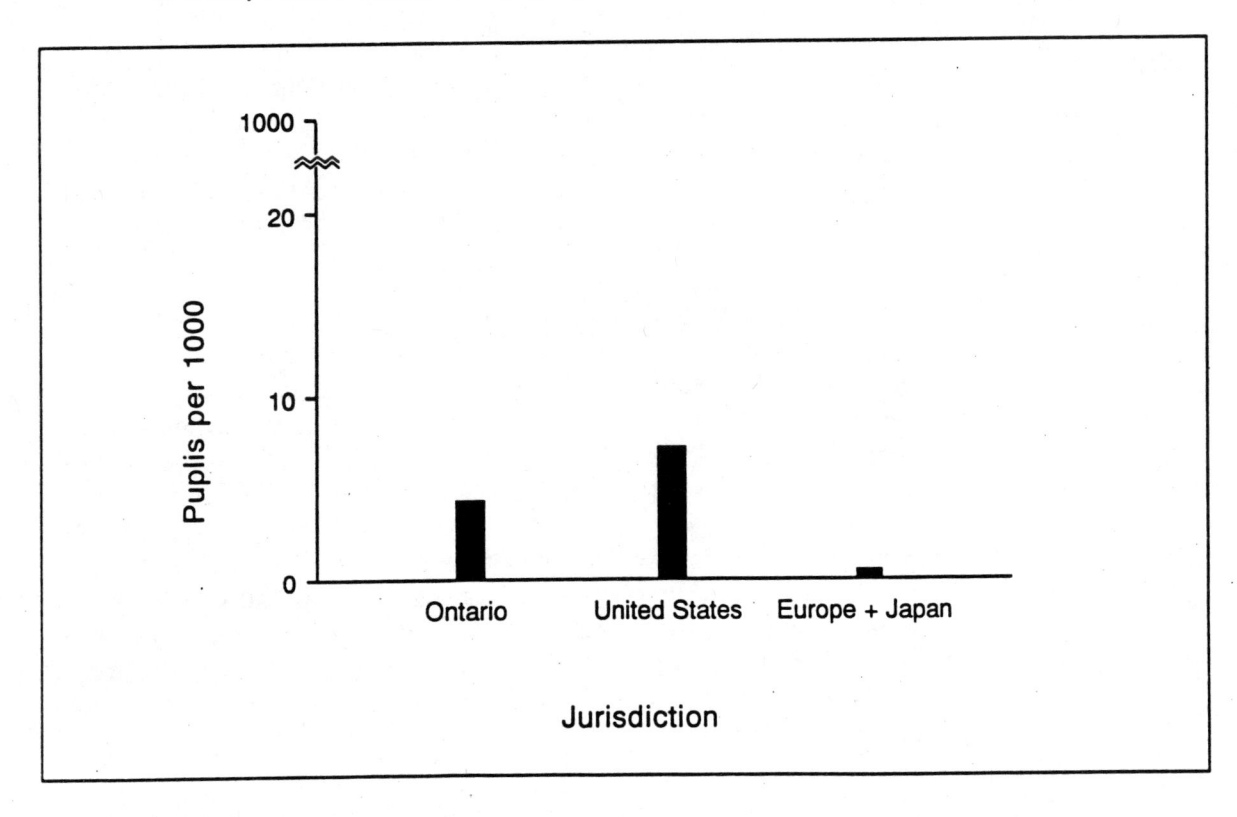

Cost Analysis

Is a cost analysis for services for the two exceptionalities available?

Of the 107 respondents, only 6 public boards and 1 separate board indicated that a cost analysis for the two exceptionalities was available.

Contractual Arrangements

Does your Board have any contractual arrangements with any other Ministry for services for the two exceptionalities?

The number of boards having contractual arrangements with another ministry is relatively small, as detailed below.

a. Developmentally Challenged students:
Six public and two separate boards have arrangements with the Ministry of Health. Seven public and two separate boards have arrangements with the Ministry of Community and Social Services. One public board has arrangements with the Ministry of Correctional Services. Five public and one separate board have arrangements with other ministries.

b. Behaviour-Disordered students:
Ten public and three separate boards contract with the Ministry of Health. Twenty-five public and nine separate boards contract with the Ministry of Community and Social Services. Ten public boards contract with the Ministry of Correctional Services. Six public and one separate board contract with other ministries.

Support Personnel

What Board employees or other agencies are available to assist behaviour-disordered and developmentally challenged pupils?

Social workers were indicated as available to both populations in this study in 61 of the 65 public boards and in 38 of the 41 separate boards. Four additional boards indicated that they or agencies in their communities provided social work services for children with behaviour disorders but not for the developmentally challenged; these boards were located in the Northeastern (two public and one separate) and Northwestern regions (one public board). The three boards in which social work services were completely unavailable are small rural boards in the Central region, one public and two separate.

The services of psychologists were available to pupils with both exceptionalities in 61 of the 65 public and 39 of the 41 separate school boards. Three additional boards (all public – one each in the Central, Northwestern, and Western regions) indicated that psychologists were available to work with behaviour-disordered pupils, but not those with developmental challenges. Conversely, one small, rural public board in the Eastern region responded that there was a psychologist available for consultation with developmentally challenged, but not behaviour-disordered pupils. Two small, rural separate boards (one Western region, one Central region) indicated that psychologists were unavailable to work with children displaying either exceptionality. However, psychometrists were available in all of the boards where pupils of either or both exceptionality had no access to psychologists. (These data were collected prior to the 1993 legislative changes that mandated the status of psychological associate in Ontario. Therefore, our data do not indicate how many of the psychometrists would qualify for this new professional designation).

The responses received indicated that psychiatrists were available in the majority of boards, although there were more exceptions than were indicated for the other professions mentioned in the survey. Availability to pupils of both exceptionalities was indicated by 56 of the 65 public and 24 of the 41 separate boards. In addition, two public and seven separate boards indicated that psychiatrists were available to serve the developmentally challenged only, while four additional public and three additional separate boards reported that psychiatrists were available to serve pupils with behavioural disorders only. The boards in which psychiatrists were reported as unavailable were located in all regions, and varied widely in size and proximity to large urban centres. In most cases, the services of psychiatrists had been arranged with outside agencies.

Speech pathologists were available to the developmentally challenged pupils in 106 of 107 responding boards, and to behaviour-disordered pupils in 103 boards. The few boards indicating gaps in service were small in size and located in rural areas. Speech correction teachers were available to work with pupils with both exceptionalities in 82 of the 107 responding boards. Developmentally challenged pupils had access to the services of speech correction teachers in four additional boards, while one board had made arrangements for speech correction teachers to work with behaviour-disordered, but not developmentally challenged children. There were only two boards reporting that pupils with both exceptionalities had no access to the assistance of either speech pathologists or speech correction teachers. There was only one board, a small separate board in the Central region, that reported no arrangements for either speech pathologists or speech correction teachers to serve pupils with either handicap.

Physical therapists were available to provide support to developmentally challenged pupils in 61 of the 65 public boards and 38 of the 41 separate boards that responded, and in the Metro Board. The seven boards where physical therapy services were unavailable were from across the province; all but two were in rural areas. Occupational therapists were available to the developmentally challenged pupils in all boards except six, including five in Northern Ontario. There were only three boards where developmentally challenged pupils had access to neither physical nor occupational therapists, one each in the Central, Mid-Northern and Northwestern regions. Nurses were available in 105 of the 107 responding boards.

Teacher-consultants were available to assist teachers in programming for the developmentally challenged in all boards except four. Teacher consultation was available regarding the needs of behaviourally-disordered pupils in all boards except five. The boards not reporting this service were scattered throughout the rural areas of the province. Guidance counsellors were available to advise on behaviour disorders in 63 of the 65 public boards and in 35 of the 41 separate boards; their services were available to the developmentally challenged pupils in about 80 per cent of the responding boards. There were three boards indicating that neither teacher-consultants nor guidance counsellors were available — all small boards in Northern sections of the province.

There were only three boards indicating that they did not provide services in more than three of the categories of professional service indicated in our survey. All were small, rural boards. Two of these were separate boards in the North; the third was a separate board in the Central region.

Conclusions: Prevalence Rates

It appears that for the 123 Ontario school boards that responded to the survey there is a considerable variance in proportions of pupils identified as behaviour disordered and developmentally challenged. Concomitantly, the fluctuations among Ontario boards and regions in terms of placement options for both groups are extremely large and cannot be explained solely by prevalence rates reported.

Cross-cultural comparisons of the proportions of children identified as developmentally delayed and as having attention deficits have repeatedly indicated prevalence rates higher in the United States than in Europe. Our data suggest that Ontario falls somewhere in between. It is recalled that identifying a pupil as exceptional may be based on a combination of the pupil's characteristics, the service delivery system (i.e., does identification facilitate access), and the means of reporting (e.g., responses to one's own government influenced by a desire to attract attention to gaps in service). It is clearly impossible to determine which of these factors affected responses to our survey. Obviously Ontario boards' responses to a study commissioned by the Ontario Ministry of Education could be seen as less independent of respondent motivation than our other replies. However, we consider the fact that the prevalence rates in Ontario fall between those of the U.S. and Europe as support for the confidence with which these data may be interpreted.

A meaningful qualitative analysis of the service of support personnel is not possible by means of questionnaires sent to school boards. However, few concerns were raised about the nature of support services in our focus groups (see Sections 4 and 6). There were many concerns expressed about the length of waiting lists and, especially in Northern and rural boards, the inaccessibility of certain needed services.

The proportions of pupils identified as behaviour disordered and developmentally challenged in Ontario seem to be somewhat lower than in the United States, but somewhat higher than in the overseas countries. Because of the disparity among definitions, it is not possible to conclusively establish the reasons for this.

Support personnel of varying types are available in almost all reporting boards. However, the data did not indicate how much time such personnel were able to devote to the two groups of exceptional pupils. For school boards that did not indicate the availability of specific types of assistance, it may be worthwhile for the Ministry of Education to help work out additional supporting arrangements.

Canadian Definitions: Developmental Challenge

The following are the main features of Canadian definitions of developmental challenge or trainable mental retardation.

Ontario

Title: Trainable mentally retarded*
- Slow intellectual development
- Ability to profit from a special program
- Limited independent social adjustment

British Columbia
- not provided

---

* Terminology used in the time of data collection.

Newfoundland
Title: Trainable retarded
(for administrative purposes only)

Alberta
Title: Trainable mentally handicapped
- Ability to profit from a special program
- Limited independent social adjustment
- Requires constant and continuous supervision for life

New Brunswick
Title: Exceptional students
(Bill 85)

Manitoba
Title: Trainable mentally handicapped
- not provided

Saskatchewan
Title: Trainable mentally retarded
- Limited independent social adjustment
- IQ below 50 +5*

Prince Edward Island
Title: Trainable mentally retarded
(for administrative purposes only)

Northwest Territories
Title: Special needs students

Canadian Definitions: Behaviour Disordered

The following are the main features of Canadian definitions of behaviour disordered.

Ontario
Title: Behaviour Disordered
A qualitatively mild, moderate, or severe learning disorder characterized by specific behaviour problems over time and of such a nature as to adversely affect the educational performance characterized by:
- Inability to build and maintain personal relationships
- Excessive fears and anxieties
- Tendency to compulsive reaction
- Inability to learn – not due to intellectual, sensory, or health factors

---

* From the original document. We assume this means a confidence interval of 5 IQ points below or above the cut-off score.

British Columbia

Title: Behaviour Disordered

Specific behaviour problems over time and of such a nature as to adversely affect the educational performance, characterized by:
- Inability to build and maintain personal relationships
- Excessive fears and anxieties
- Social problems, e.g., delinquency, substance abuse, child abuse
- Behaviour differs significantly from age-appropriate expectations
- Intense or frequent problem behaviours
- Uncontrolled aggression and/or hyperactivity
- Behaviours related to other disabling conditions

Newfoundland

Title: Behaviour Disordered
(for administrative purposes only)

Alberta

Title: Behaviour Disordered

A qualitatively mild, moderate, or severe learning disorder characterized by specific behaviour problems over time and of such a nature as to adversely affect the educational performance, characterized by:
- Inability to build and maintain personal relationships
- Excessive fears and anxieties
- Uncontrolled aggression and/or hyperactivity
- General mood of unhappiness or depression
- Inappropriate behaviour or feelings under ordinary conditions
- Difficulty in accepting realities of personal responsibility and accountability

New Brunswick

Behavioural exceptionality
No definition was specified in New Brunswick's response.
(Bill 85)

Manitoba

No definition was given in Manitoba's response.

Saskatchewan

Title: Socially, emotionally (behaviourally) disabled. A pupil may be identified as high-cost socially, emotionally, or behaviourally disabled* "when a thorough diagnostic study by medical and educational personnel acceptable to the minister affirms that the pupil exhibits excessive, chronic deviant behaviour which adversely affects educational performance." (Regulation 49 (g)). Pupils identified under the category of socially, emotionally (behaviourally) disabled will exhibit excessive, chronic, deviant behaviours. Some students will be aggressive, destructive, impulsive, or anti-social; others may be depressed or withdrawn. More severely disordered pupils may demonstrate bizarre and inappropriate behaviours such as self-injury, crying, and debilitating feelings of inferiority.

---

* Terminology used in original documents

Prince Edward Island

The response from this province indicated that emotionally/behaviourally disordered children are those who cannot function in a class without distracting all therein, exhibiting aggressive/hurtful behaviour towards other children, and generally making it almost impossible for a teacher to work with the children without continual interruption. Most behaviourally/emotionally disturbed children at the elementary level are assigned a one-to-one teacher assistant who works with them.

Overseas Definitions: Trainable Retarded or Developmentally Challenged

The following are the main features of overseas definitions of trainable retarded or behaviour disordered.

Sweden

Title: Mentally retarded
- Inhibited intellectual development
- Requires special educational program
- Social adjustment problems

Denmark

Title: (no definition – "normalization")

Finland

Title: Moderately mentally handicapped
(no definition provided)

The Netherlands

Title: Mentally handicapped
- Inhibited intellectual development
- Difficult to educate
- Requires special schools

England

Title: Special educational needs students
(no definition provided)

Germany

Title: Mentally handicapped
- Inhibited intellectual development
- Emotional differences
- Lack of ability of expression
- Motor deficiencies
- Communication deficits

Switzerland

Title: Mentally deficient
- Inhibited intellectual development
- Lack of ability of expression
- Motor deficiencies
- IQ 55-60

Ireland
Title: Moderately mentally handicapped
- Inhibited intellectual development
- Requires special educational program
- Requires constant pedagogical attention
- IQ 25-50

Japan
Title: Moderately mentally handicapped
- Inhibited intellectual development
- IQ 75
- Limited speech communication, speech to some extent
- Limited care of self
- Limited social life with assistance

Australia – South Australia, Queensland, Tasmania, Northern Territory
(no definitions provided)

South Africa
Title: Mentally retarded
- Inhibited intellectual development
- IQ 30-50

Overseas Definitions: Behaviour Disordered

The following are the main features of overseas definitions of behaviour disordered.

Sweden
Title: Behaviour disordered and adjustment difficulties
- Difficulty adjusting to rules
- Open aggression (extraversion)
- Severe inhibition (introversion)
- Variety of behaviour patterns: anxiety, destructiveness, distraction, inattention, usually in combination
- Behaviour disturbance affects performance in school and in the environment

Denmark
Title: Behaviour Disordered
(no definition provided)

Finland
Title: Emotionally and socially maladjusted
(no definition provided)

The Netherlands
Title: Learning and Behaviour Disordered
- Does not make progress in ordinary schools
- Very vulnerable and nervous, but of normal intelligence
- Severely maladjusted
- Learning and behaviour difficulties

England
Title: Children with special education needs
(no definition provided)

Germany
Title: Behaviour Disordered
- Severe inhibition
- Variety of behaviour patterns: anxiety, destructiveness, distraction, inattention, usually in combination
- Excessive shyness
- Lack of control

Switzerland
Title: Behaviourally deficient
- Difficulty adjusting to rules
- Behaviour disturbance affects performance in school and in the environment
- Behaviour deviates from the norm
- Behaviour endangers own life or other persons and possessions

Ireland
Title: Behaviour disordered
(no definition provided)

Japan
Title: Emotionally disturbed (2 groups)
- Open aggression
- Severe inhibition (autistic)

South Africa
Title: Emotionally disturbed/Behaviour deviation
(no definition provided)

Australia
Northern Territory – label-free

Tasmania
Title: Behaviour of serious concern
- Behaviour disturbance affects performance in school and in the environment
- Excessive shyness
- Behaviour inappropriate in social situations, interferes significantly with student's or others' well-being, learning, etc.
- Behaviour continues subsequent to appropriate intervention.

Conclusions: Definitional Issues

As indicated in the above summaries, there are important conceptual differences among the definitions. In the case of developmental challenge, there is considerable division among the jurisdictions with regard to the core features of the definition. Many provinces and countries conceptualize developmental challenge in terms of delay in intellectual development. This is a relatively traditional approach, though it is important to note that specific IQ limits have become less common. Other jurisdictions have emphasized impaired adaptation to the social environment. This feature has become more prevalent in psychiatric nomenclature in recent years. An inability to profit from regular schooling is a feature of the working definitions of developmental challenge/trainable retardation in several jurisdictions.

There were a number of overlapping themes in the definitions of behaviour disorder. Several definitions were focused on the inability to form or maintain satisfying interpersonal relationships. Others contained the provision that the problem behaviour must be infrequent for the child's age. In some cases, the problems must be sufficient to interfere with the child's own learning. Others specified that the problems must interfere with the learning environments or well-being of others. Many definitions featured examples of specific problem behaviours; these varied considerably. Tasmania's definition contained the provision that the problem behaviour must persist after appropriate intervention. This provision may be useful in reducing unnecessary identification.

Understandably, all definitions focused on concepts rather than objective yardsticks for specifying the behaviours to be included. Therefore, it is difficult to establish the degree to which these discrepancies in definition are accountable for the different rates of identification of children as behaviour disordered or developmentally challenged. In order to establish a common framework for our discussions throughout the province, this research team presented hypothetical case descriptions as stimuli for all focus groups, as reported in Sections 4 and 6.

Reference

Magliocca, L.A., and Stephens, T.M. (1980). Child identification or child inventory? A critique of the federal design of child identification systems implemented under PL 94-142. **Journal of Special Education, 14**, 23-36.

SECTION 3

EDUCATIONAL ENVIRONMENTS FOR THE BEHAVIOUR-DISORDERED PUPIL: A "BEST EVIDENCE" SYNTHESIS

ABSTRACT

The nature of the optimal educational environment for pupils with behaviour disorders is a matter of considerable controversy. This report is a quantitative summary of research conducted in several countries in which different special education settings — regular class, resource room, special class, special school, and others — are compared in terms of their impact on the functioning of these youngsters.

There are many limitations in reviewing this literature and in comparing the ten studies. These are fully explored and discussed within this section. The review acknowledged that the objective of the researchers was to be based on the "best evidence" of the best designed studies only.

The results of the synthesis are explored under the areas of overall setting effects, publication bias, sampling procedure, age effects, academic achievement, self-concept, and behavioural improvement. The authors conclude their study with several clear implications: first, that behaviour-disordered youngsters require more support than is available to the regular class teacher, who is often unassisted by resource personnel, and secondly, that it appears that most behaviour-disordered youngsters will require ongoing support for a number of years, since special programs do not seem, on the whole, to permanently "cure" behavioural exceptionalities and permit full re-integration for the youngster's school career.

Less clear findings were reported with regard to the choice of special program for youngsters with behaviour disorders. The authors conclude by noting that educational planning would be greatly facilitated by more comprehensive research that would take into account the setting, the program, the teacher, and the behavioural profile of the individual pupil.

The nature of the optimal educational environment for pupils with behaviour disorders is a matter of considerable controversy. Extensive research has been conducted on the effectiveness of intervention procedures for these youngsters (see reviews by Carpenter and Apter, 1988, Nelson and Rutherford, 1988, and Wood, 1990). While it is possible to conduct most commonly used interventions in "regular" as well as "special" settings, there are a number of obstacles, including cost and limitations in both staff training and time (Wood, 1990). Professionals working with behaviour-disordered children often participate in decisions regarding the degree of restrictiveness appropriate to the children's needs. This report examines the research basis for such decisions.

Challenges in Reviewing Literature

Problems are inherent in comparing diverse studies on any topic. Educational and psychological researchers have given increased attention to the many obstacles confronted when one tries to develop a "bottom line" conclusion about the collective results of a series of studies in any given area. The reader interested in a more detailed discussion of procedures and pitfalls in reviewing research is referred to Light and Pillemer's (1984) very readable volume or Schneider's (1991) chapter on the subject. Among the problems is the fact that different studies explore different variables (e.g., self-concept, academic achievement, aggression), using different measures or tests whose numerical values are not readily comparable. Another problem is that all studies are not of equivalent value or relevance to the reviewer's purpose – some are conducted with larger sample sizes, others with too few; some use valid tests and measures; others do not, etc. As well, the reviewer may not attend to all features of the study or portray them accurately in the review, but may be excessively influenced by the author's discussion rather than actual data, or may select certain results, ignoring others (e.g., in a study that includes both variables, attention may be focused on results affecting academic achievement but not classroom behaviour, or vice versa). For this and other reasons, it is quite possible for two reviewers of the same literature to come up with diametrically opposed conclusions about what it says (see, for example, Light and Pillemer's 1984 comparison of two conflicting reviews of the literature on the outcomes of compensatory early education programs for at-risk preschoolers).

Problems Specific to This Literature

In addition to the general considerations discussed above, there are certain specific challenges in reviewing this group of studies. One of these is the lack of suitable control groups. In theory, it would be desirable to compare children who receive one type of special programming with an equivalent, randomly assigned group who received another form of assistance, given the fact that it would be unethical to provide no help to pupils in need. However, this is rarely possible. While non-random assignment of subjects, where necessary, is acceptable in research, the pupils must be equivalent in the settings compared. Placement decisions are usually made by parents, teachers, and professionals based on their perceptions of where the individual pupil would be best placed, as is legally mandated in many jurisdictions. With the growing emphasis on integration, there is a tendency for youngsters having more extensive needs to be found in more restrictive settings. Therefore, many studies do not and cannot utilize fully comparable control groups. While they might compare pupils' progress in one setting with that of pupils in another, these pupils may have exceptionalities that vary enormously in nature and severity, rendering comparison of the two groups highly problematic. For these reasons, the best data available for comparing pupil progress in settings varying in integration are, unfortunately, somewhat dated.

These difficulties are exacerbated by the fact that the subjects are rarely well described in these studies. Terms such as "aggressive", "conduct disordered", "emotionally disturbed", "socially maladjusted", and the like are used in a confusing variety of ways, making it impossible to determine whether the participants in various studies are in any way similar. Smith, Wood, and Grimes (1988) discuss the implications of the lack of standard terminology in this field.

Finally, very few studies have explored the interactions of setting, program, and teacher effects. For example, a study in which special classes are compared with resource room programs would likely not differentiate among special classes in which various techniques were used (not to mention how well they were used), nor between resource rooms staffed by highly experienced or less experienced personnel. Therefore, the results of the study might not optimally portray the true potential of either type of program. In the absence of research in which setting, program, and teacher effects are comprehensively investigated, the following review focuses on studies in which different settings or placement options are compared. The reader interested in comparing various intervention techniques for the behaviour disordered is referred to a meta-analytic review of those studies by Skiba and Casey (1985).

Furthermore, researchers have paid little attention to the transient nature of this population. Most studies adopt a fixed time period for measurement of change; for example, pre-test on admission to the program, post-test six months later. In the interim, highly reticent or highly disruptive children may well have left the program, and are not included in the measurement of outcome. While methods exist for taking this "dropout effect" into account, they have rarely been used in comparing placement options for the behaviour disordered. Because of this, many studies may indicate inflated estimates of success.

Meta-Analytic Synthesis of Comparisons Between Groups

Meta-analysis is a technique developed to bring greater rigour to the science of reviewing previous studies. In conducting a meta-analysis, the reviewer must clearly indicate the source of studies reviewed (the sample) and the methods used for summarizing them. The statistics reported in the original studies are converted, no matter which statistical strategy was used in the original study, into a standard common unit known as an effect-size estimate. In this way, the effect-size estimate of one study can be compared with others, even if they have different sample sizes, used different tests, etc. Sometimes it is sufficient to report a single average effect size for a group of studies, and determine how significant it is; for instance, if one were attempting to determine whether self-contained social adjustment classes in regular schools have favourable outcomes overall. However, most reviewers would be interested in reporting greater detail, perhaps comparing effect sizes for older children with younger ones, outcomes for self-concept with outcomes for anxiety, outcomes for special classes in regular schools with completely separate special schools, etc. Therefore, most meta-analytic reviews report and compare a number of effect-size estimates. These meta-analytic techniques were used by Calberg and Kavale (1980) in their review of the effects of special and regular classes. However, that review is by now quite dated, and focused primarily on children with learning rather than behaviour disorders.

Two types of data are useful in evaluating change in pupil behaviour and achievement that ensues from any program, treatment or placement. The first is within-groups change, e.g., changes in pupil scores after participation in a program. Most other meta-analyses have focused exclusively on this type of data. They have typically calculated an effect size for each experimental group in each study, as well as an effect size for each control group in each study. The mean effect size for the experimental groups is then compared with the corresponding statistic for the control groups. As discussed above, combining and averaging the effect sizes for the highly heterogeneous groups in the current data base would be highly problematic.

For these reasons, the second, or meta-analytic, strategy, was used in this study. It consisted of a meta-analytic synthesis of between-groups comparisons. This has the advantage of maintaining the distinctness of each study to a greater degree than in traditional meta-analysis, permitting each experimental group to be compared to its own control group, whose subjects should be most comparable. Readers interested in comparing the results of this review with other quantitative literature reviews must bear this fundamental difference in mind.

Method

A "Best Evidence" Synthesis

As mentioned above, not all studies on a given topic are of equal quality and usefulness. In contrast with several well-designed studies, results of others are virtually impossible to interpret because: (1) subjects are so poorly described that it is questionable whether to include them under the general rubric "behaviour-disordered"; (2) program and setting descriptions are so sketchy that they cannot be characterized in the most general terms such as resource room, regular class, special class, etc.; (3) outcome measures are highly subjective, such as unstandardized ratings of improvement by persons involved in delivering the program; or (4) there is no comparison group at all. Our first decision, then, was that our review would be based on the "best evidence" (Slavin, 1987) available, that is, the results of the best designed studies only, in contrast with a review of the vast number of studies available, which provide data of lesser value.

Literature Search and Inclusion Rules

Thorough computer searches were conducted of the following data bases: Psychological Abstracts, ERIC documents, and Dissertation Abstracts International. However, we recognized that relevant articles might be overlooked by this procedure, because of the above-mentioned confusion in the terminology used to describe subjects. Therefore, once a relevant document was found, its bibliography was scanned for other relevant references. While several hundred interesting articles were located, most of these were program descriptions or theoretical discussions without any evaluative data.

In order to present conclusions based on the "best evidence" available, the following criteria were set for studies to be included in the final sample:

1. The study (or an identifiable portion) had to be conducted with behaviour disordered, emotionally disturbed, or aggressive pupils in at least one of the following types of setting: regular class, resource room (or resource/withdrawal), self-contained special class, separate special school, treatment centre, or hospital.

2. The study had to compare changes in these youngsters with those of a population of behaviour-disordered, emotionally disturbed, or aggressive youngsters in a second type of setting; the control or comparison group had to be similar in age.

3. The study had to report changes in the participants' academic achievement, behaviour, or self-concept in a quantitative manner suitable for meta-analysis.

Since these criteria were most applicable to the assessment of short-term gain, we decided to summarize studies that had included long-term follow-up measurement separately; this necessitated a less stringent set of inclusion criteria, for several reasons. The results of the follow-up studies are presented separately at the end of this section.

Coding of Studies

Each study was independently coded by two research assistants with bachelor's degrees in psychology. They coded a total of 11 categories: diagnostic description of subjects, sample size, age, IQ, sex distribution, type of control group, method of assigning subjects to groups, source of outcome data (e.g., pupil, teacher, direct observation), dependent variable, teacher experience, and teacher strategy or treatment technique used. The two latter categories were dropped because of insufficient data. The two raters agreed exactly on 86 per cent of the individual coding decisions, and no coding category had inter-rater agreement less than 80 per cent.

Results

Overview

A graphic presentation has been used to facilitate readability. In each of the graphs on the following pages, the effect-size estimate for each study (or each setting comparison in studies that involved three or more types of setting) is assigned a bar on a histogram. Please note that an effect-size estimate known as r (Rosenthal, 1984) was used in this study. There are several other types of effect-size statistics (delta, d, g, etc.). Therefore, the magnitudes of the effect cannot be compared with effect sizes from other meta-analyses if they have used other effect-size estimate statistics (however, these can be easily transformed).

Each bar represents the comparison between change estimates for two settings. For example, the first bar at the left in Figure 3.1 describes a comparison between changes of behaviour-disordered pupils in regular classes and in special classes. Where the more restrictive setting (in this case, it could have been the special classes) has the higher effect size, the bar is drawn above the dividing line. However, in the study by Calhoun and Elliott (1977), it was determined that greater gain was made by those who remained in regular classes; therefore, the bar is drawn below the line, i.e., in favour of the less restrictive setting. It is necessary to consult the legend to determine exactly which settings are being compared. The unshaded bar for the Calhoun and Elliott study indicates that it was a comparison between regular and special classes. It is important to remember that, while the results favoured the regular classes, this does not necessarily mean that the youngsters in the special class deteriorated; it might only indicate that they did not make as much gain.

Publication Bias

In Figure 3.2, published studies are separated from unpublished research and theses. This was done because professional journals are known to be biased against studies that do not report significant findings (Light and Pillemer, 1984). Interestingly, the three studies that showed the largest effect sizes for the less restrictive of two special programs were theses. However, for each thesis finding in favour of a less restrictive setting, there was at least one other thesis with the opposite conclusion, though not as strong. Nevertheless, the results suggest that journal articles may depict an unrealistic degree of success for more restrictive programs.

Sampling Procedure

As mentioned above, many of the study findings are difficult to interpret because comparisons are made between groups of youngsters who are not very similar. This creates an a priori bias in favour of the setting in which less disturbed or deviant children participate. In Figure 3.3 the study findings are sorted according to sampling procedure. In the six studies at the left, random assignment of subjects to groups was achieved despite the obstacles discussed above. These results, therefore, inspire the most confidence. Subjects in the next group of studies were not assigned randomly to groups, but the groups appeared equivalent on the pre-test measures used. It must be remembered that, in these studies, the groups compared may well differ on some other variable not considered by the investigator. The final set of studies did not provide for random assignment. As well, the groups were known to differ in some important way. These results must be interpreted with extreme caution.

Figure 3.1
Effect Size by Setting

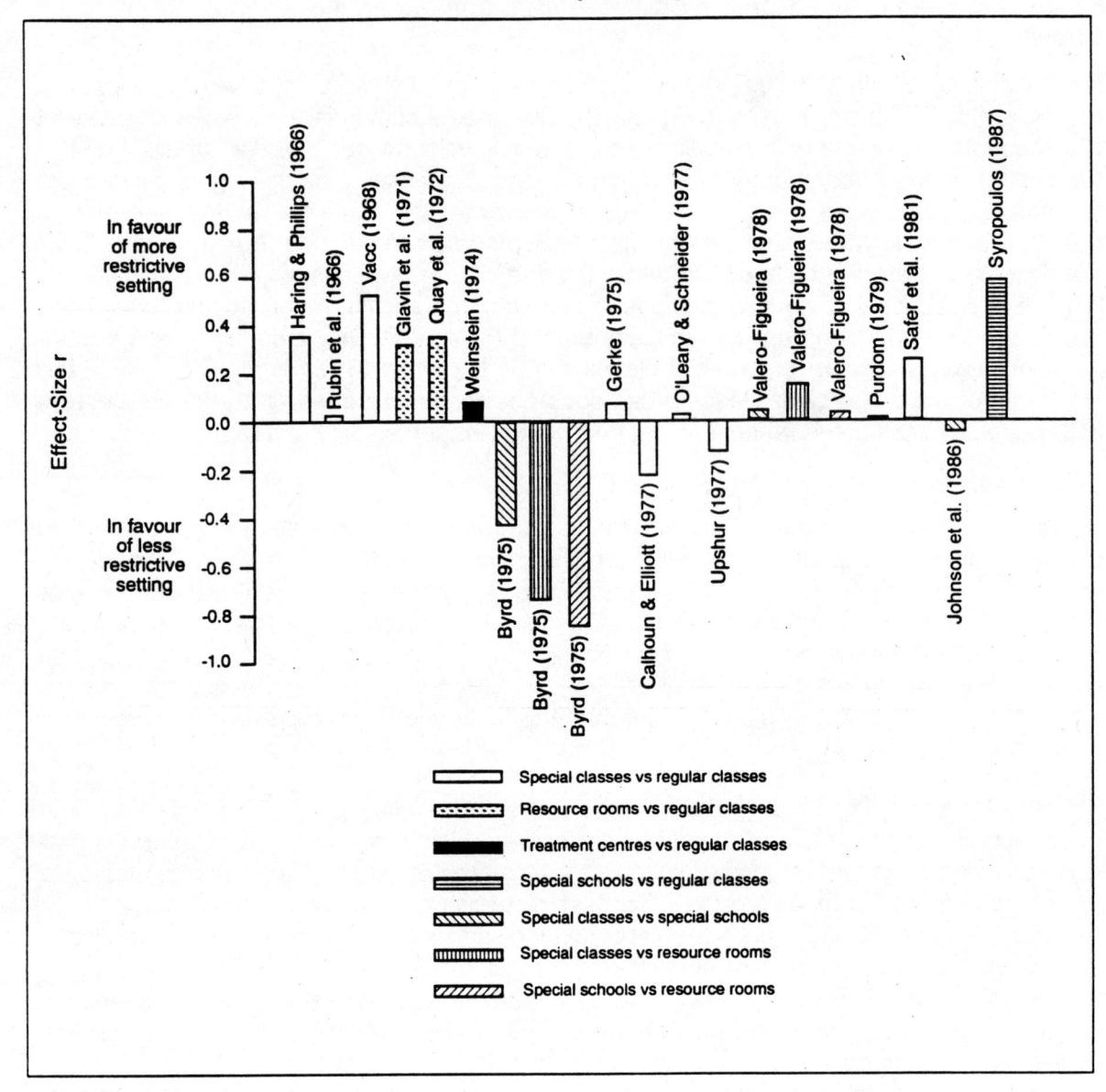

Figure 3.2
Effect Size by Publication Status

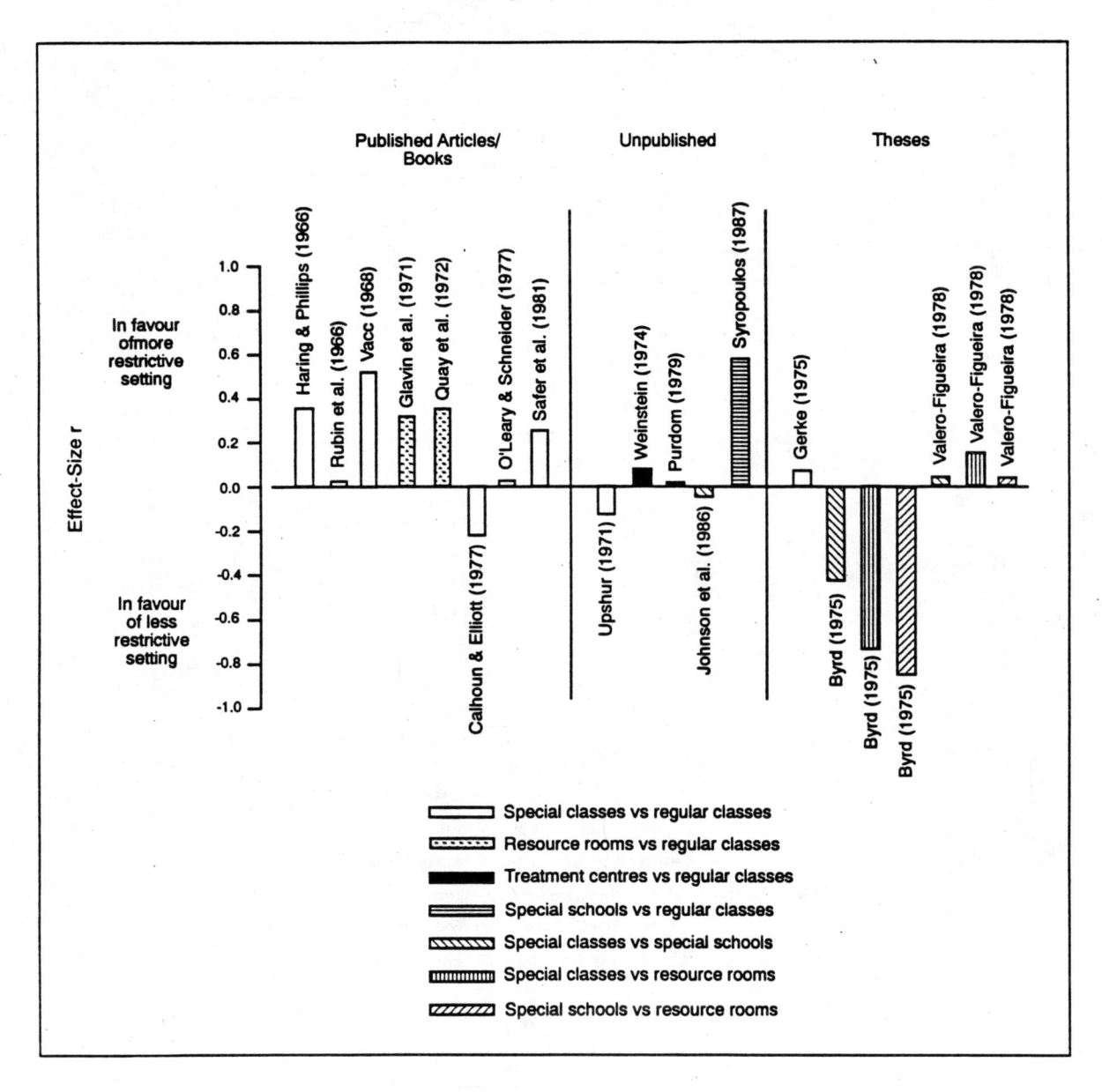

**Figure 3.3
Effect Size by Sampling Procedure**

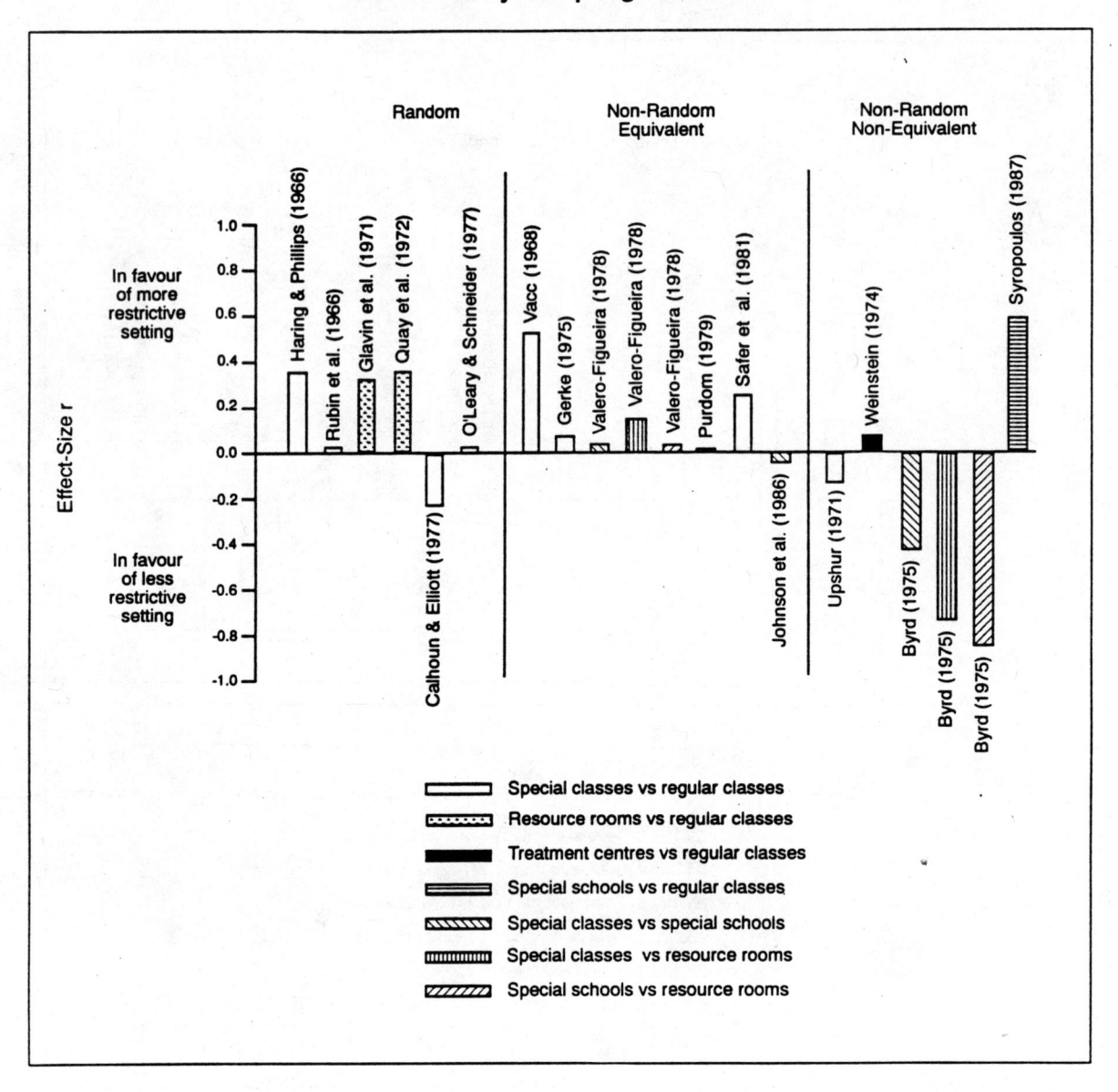

As shown, most of the findings in favour of less restrictive settings are from studies in which the groups compared were known to be different from the start. Therefore, these results must be discounted, as the youngsters in the less restrictive environments may have achieved greater gain because they were less disturbed to begin with.

Age Effects

In Figure 3.4, effect sizes are separated by the average age of subjects. As shown, there has been little research with youngsters under eight years old, and the few studies here have yielded inconclusive results. The later elementary years have received the most research attention. At this age, all special settings appeared to be more effective than regular classes, but comparisons among special programs were inconclusive. Researchers have not explored as comprehensively the effects of these programs for youngsters aged 12 years and older.

Figure 3.4
Effect Size by Mean Age

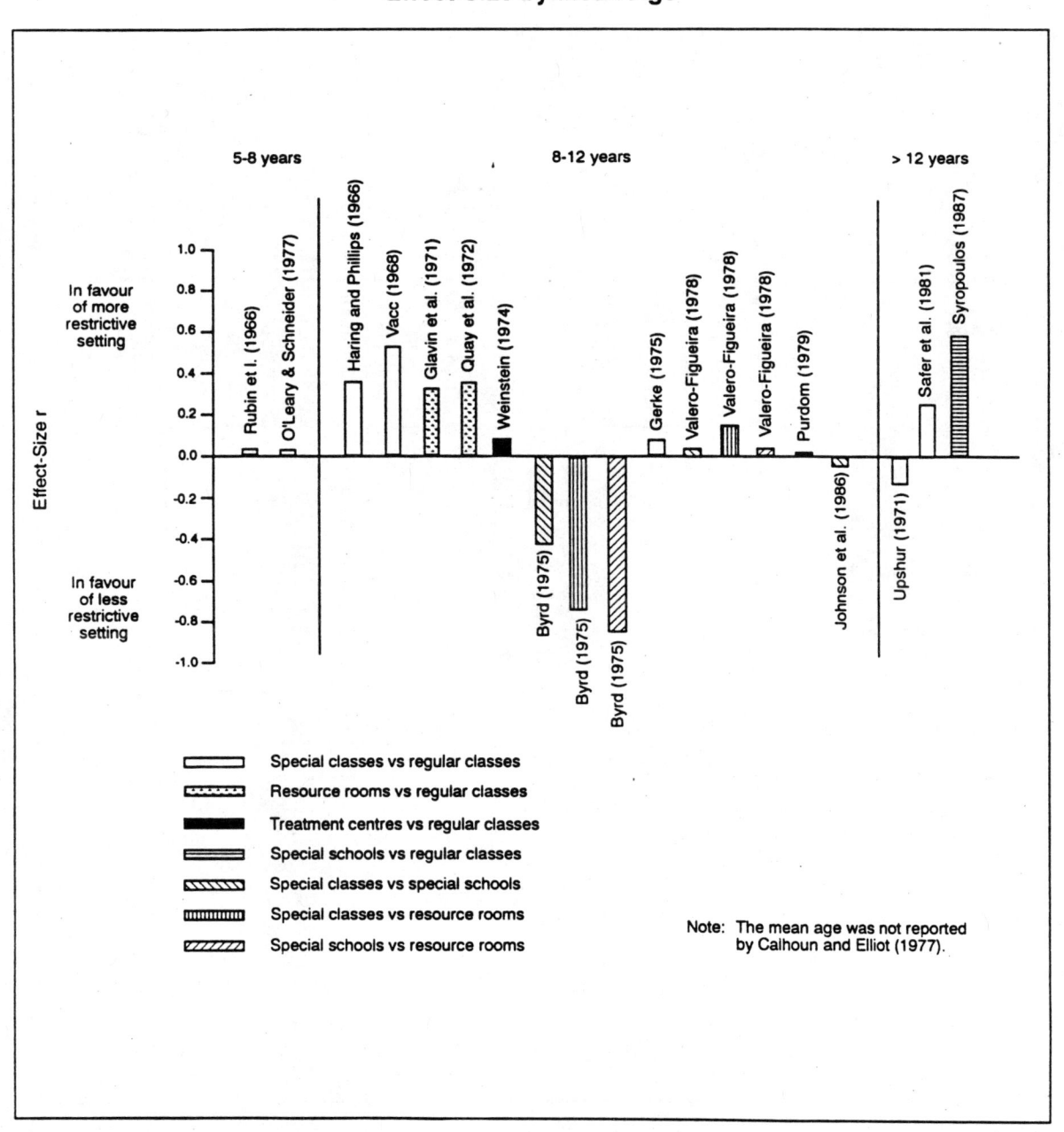

Academic Achievement

The findings discussed so far have been collapsed across dependent variables. In other words, they are a composite of results for academic achievement, behaviour, and self-concept. However, it is of considerable interest to specify setting effects on each of these dimensions. Results for measures of academic achievement are plotted in Figure 3.5. Academic achievement was included as a variable in almost all of the studies. The pattern of findings for academic achievement mirrors that for the composite effect sizes: special programs appear more effective than regular classes; comparisons among special programs are inconclusive.

Figure 3.5
Effect Sizes for Academic Achievement Measures

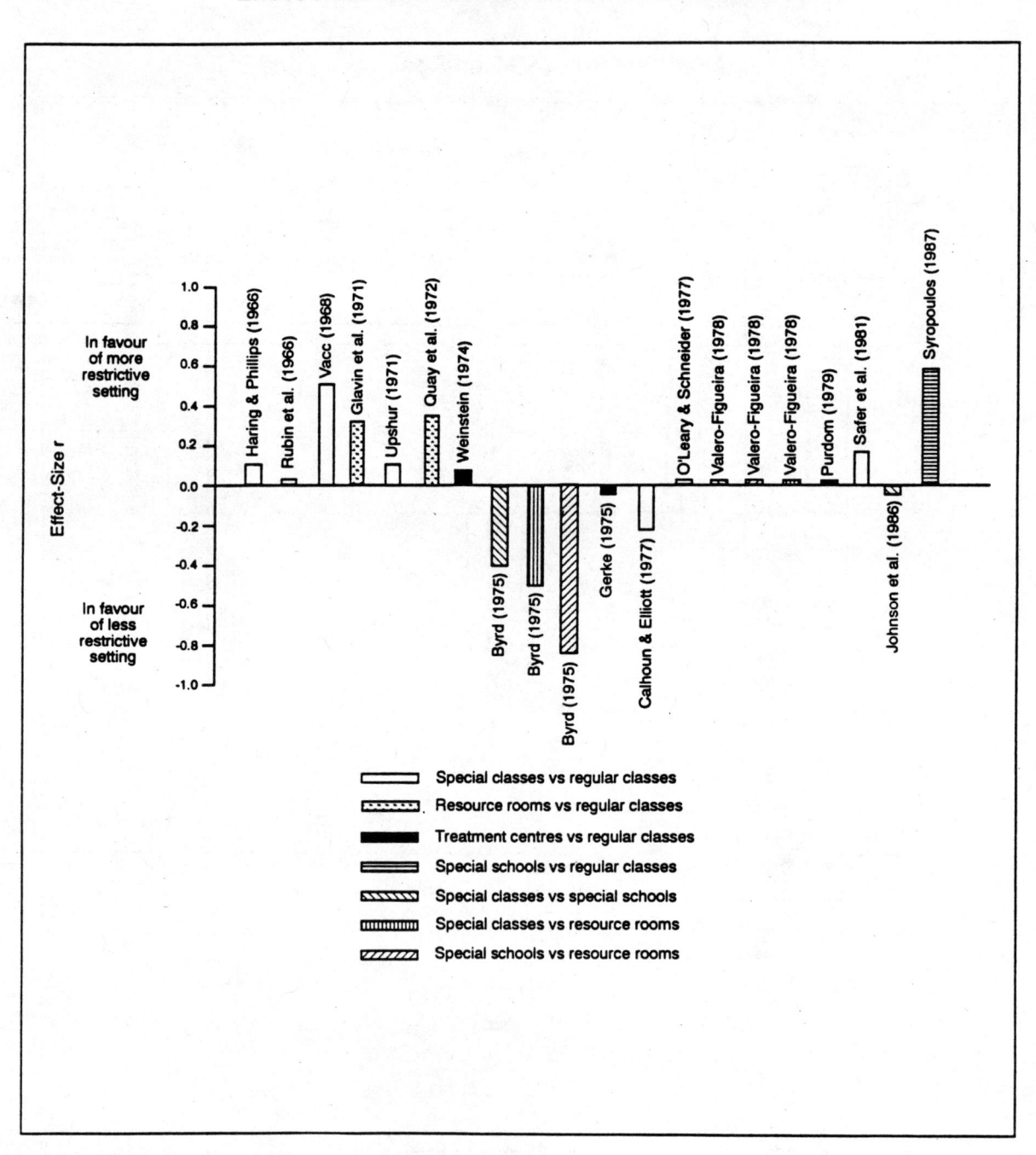

Self-Concept

The findings for self-concept portrayed in Figure 3.6 contrast sharply with the other results. There is a clear tendency for less restrictive settings to achieve better results in terms of children's self-concept.

**Figure 3.6
Effect Sizes for Self-Concept Measures**

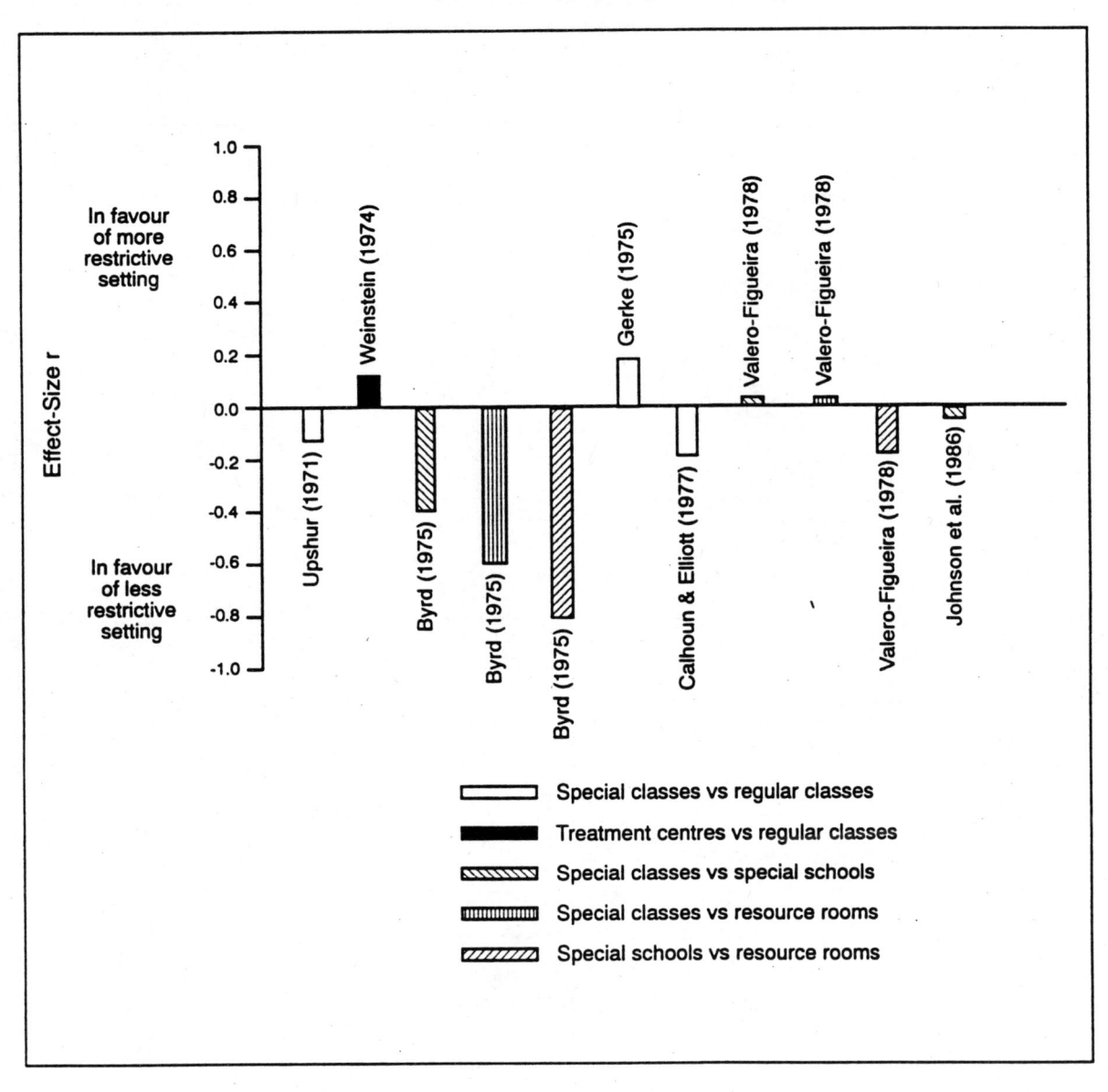

Behavioural Improvement

The next two figures portray comparisons of gain in measures of behaviour. Figure 3.7 is devoted to studies in which the investigators relied on on-site, direct observation of pupil behaviour. Unfortunately, this was done in only 6 of the 16 studies. As displayed, the results are somewhat inconclusive. Ratings by teachers and parents are more biased than observational data, since they are not "blind" – the raters know very well that the youngsters are participating in a special program and may, therefore, expect it to work. As displayed in Figure 3.8, the teacher ratings tend to portray greater effectiveness for special classes and treatment centres. Weinstein's (1974) study is interesting because it revealed totally opposite perspectives by teachers and parents with regard to the progress made by participants in the same program.

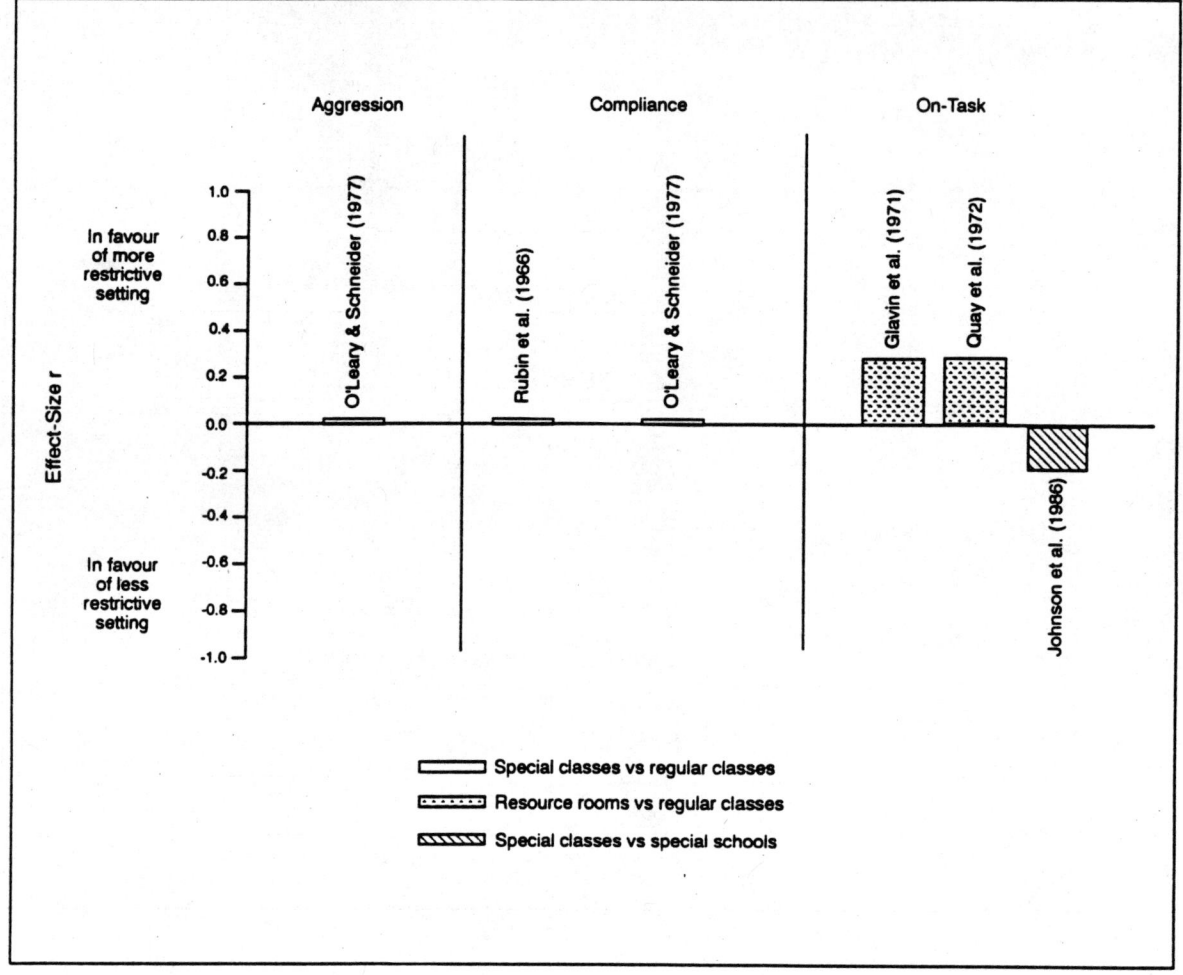

Figure 3.7
Effect Sizes for Behavioural Observations Measures

**Figure 3.8
Effect Sizes for Behavioural Rating Scales**

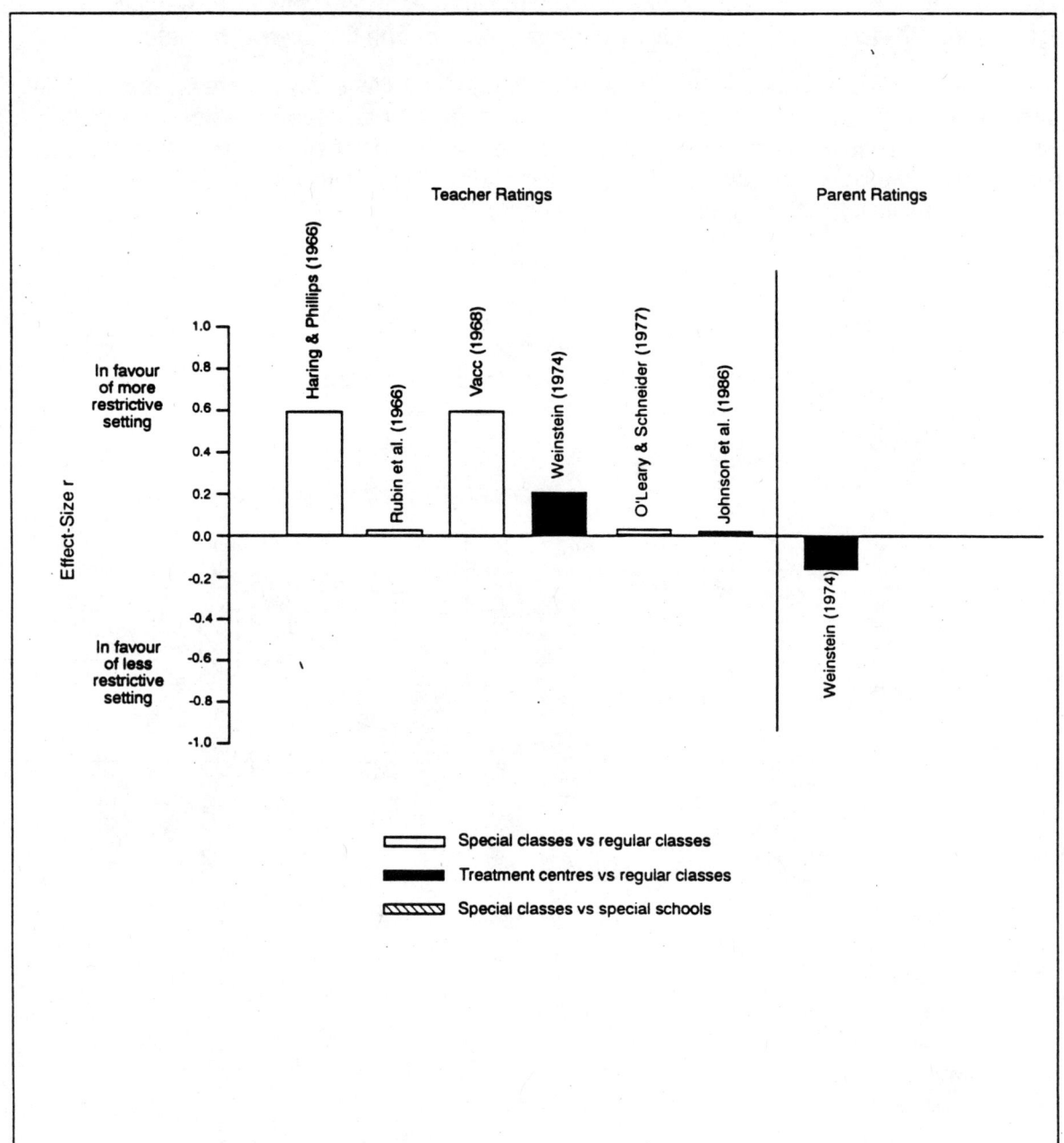

Follow-up Studies

The studies discussed above focused on short-term gain, with post-testing taking place six months to one year after pre-testing. However, the long-term impact of special programming is also of considerable interest. Follow-up studies pose methodological challenges to the researcher that are quite different from those discussed above. Foremost among these is the loss of subjects who move away, drop out of school, or discontinue participation. Furthermore, few research programs operate for more than several years. Therefore, it is rare to find long-term follow-up studies that include such relatively time-consuming procedures as special academic testing or observations of behaviour.

A different strategy was needed in order to accommodate follow-up studies in this review. Documents in the initial pool were, therefore, re-scanned for follow-up statistics as to the setting in which the subjects were being educated (i.e., did they remain in regular class? regular school? etc.) at the time of follow-up measurement one to seven years later.

The follow-up results are depicted in Figures 3.9 through 3.12. As shown, there is considerable variation among locations in terms of the proportion of participants who successfully reintegrated in regular school programs several years after discharge from special classes or schools for the behaviour disordered. However, after a number of years, only the minority appear to achieve total re-integration with success.

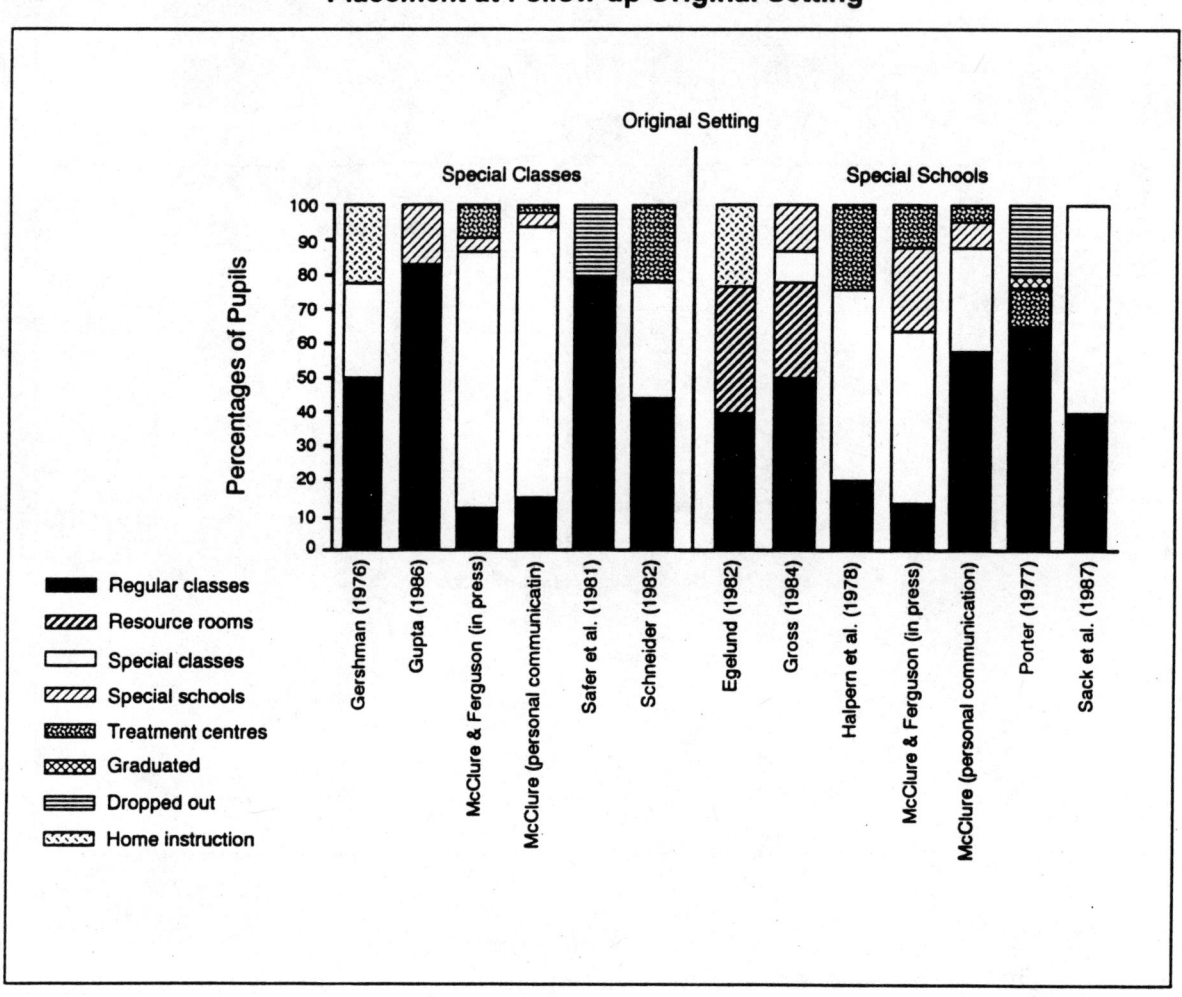

**Figure 3.9
Placement at Follow-up Original Setting**

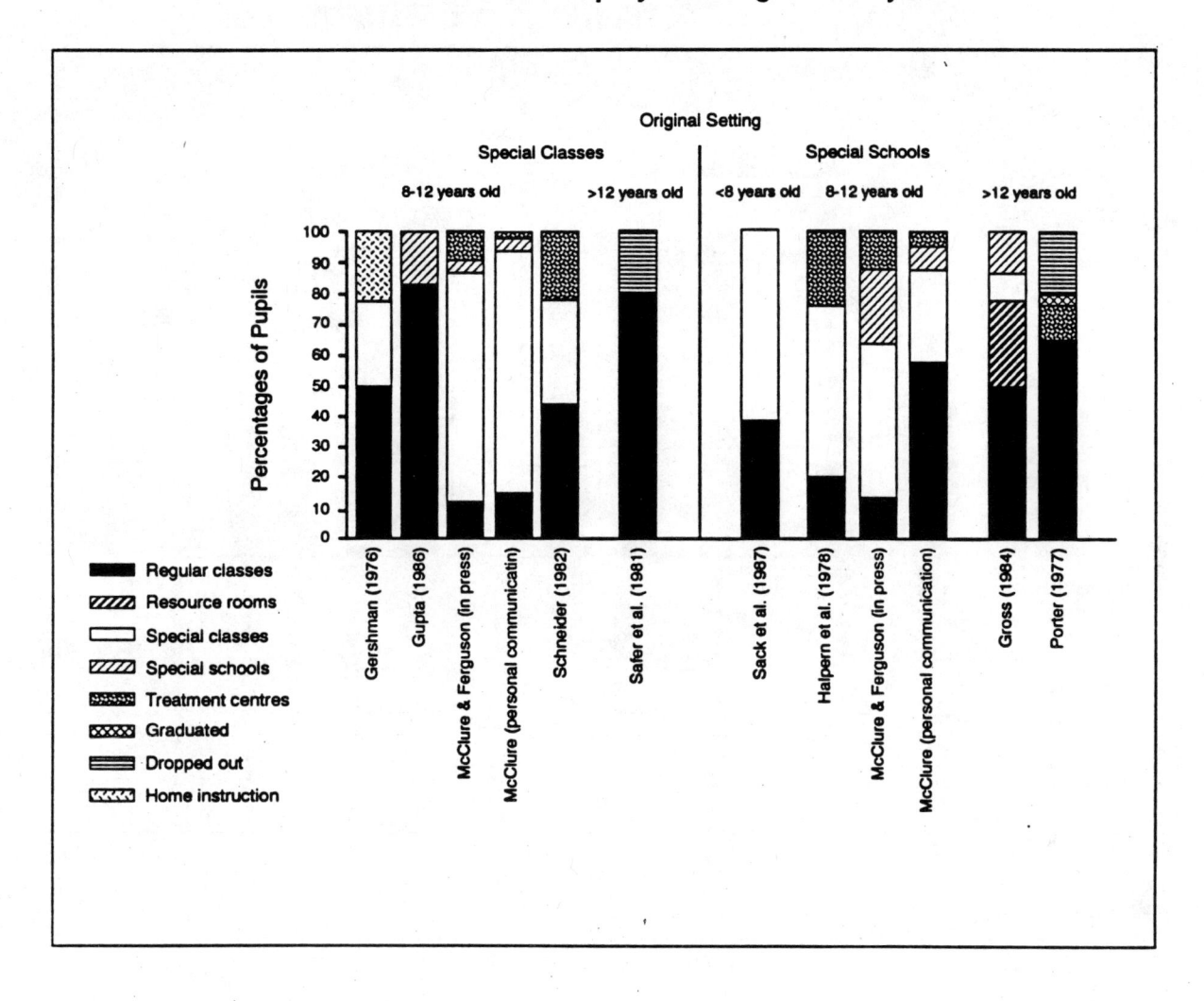

**Figure 3.10
Placement at Follow-up by Mean Age at Entry**

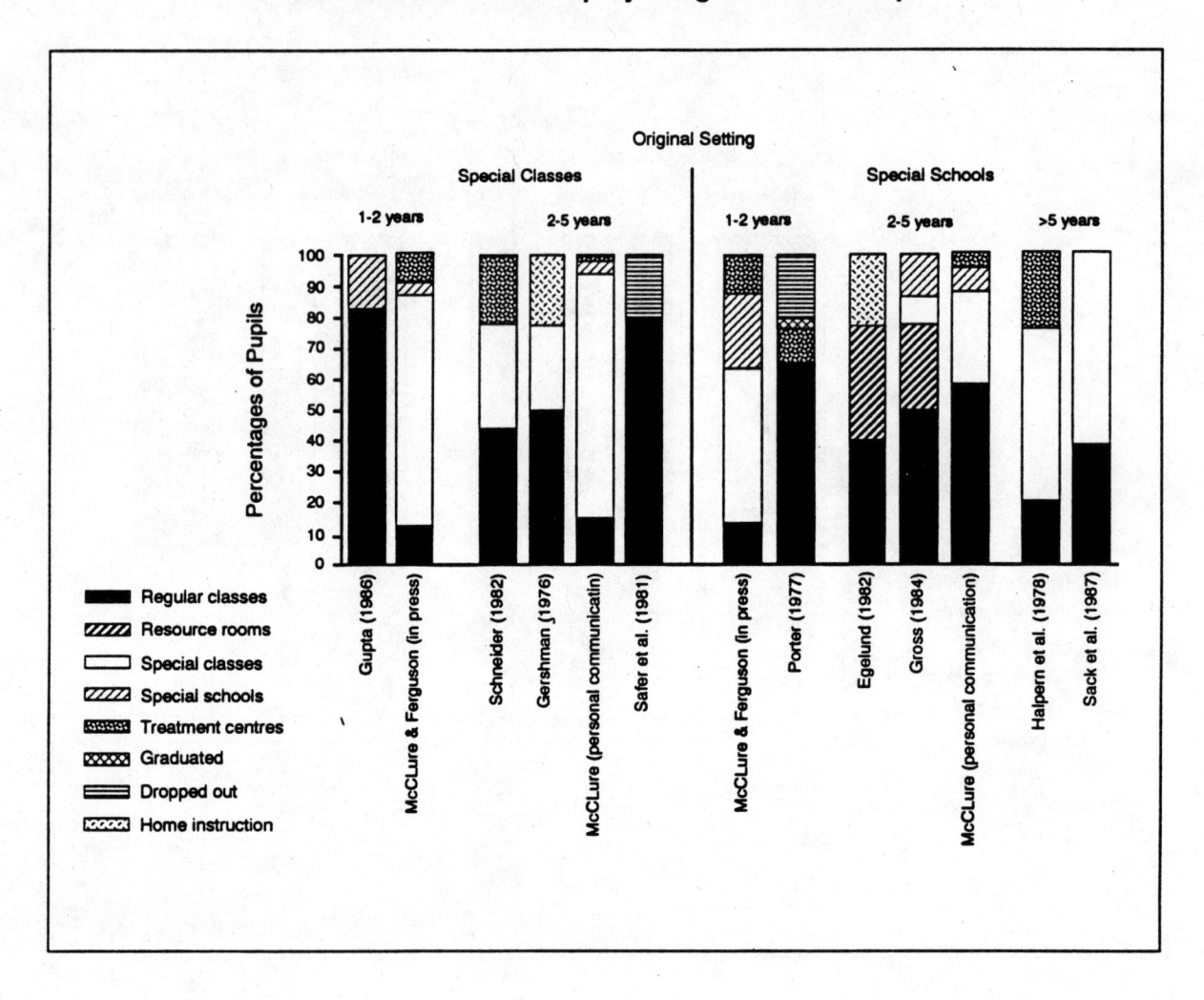

**Figure 3.11
Placement at Follow-up by Length of Follow-Up**

**Figure 3.12
Placement at Follow-up by Country**

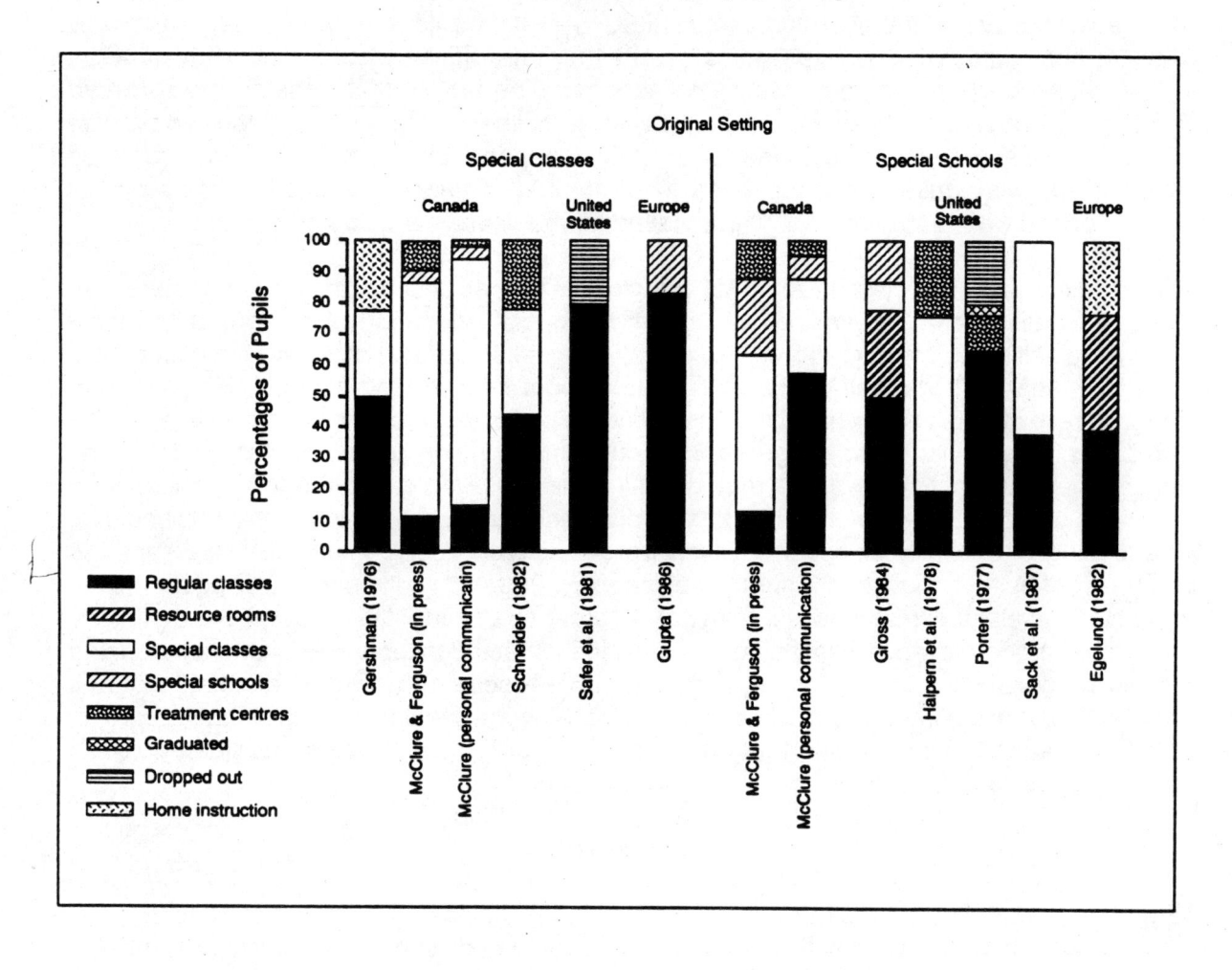

Conclusions

While we believe that these studies constitute the "best evidence" available, their many limitations, discussed above, indicate that they should be interpreted with caution. Nevertheless, there are some clear implications. The first is that behaviour-disordered youngsters require more support than is available to the regular class teacher unassisted by at least resource room personnel. Secondly, it appears that most behaviour-disordered youngsters will require ongoing support for a number of years: special programs do not seem, on the whole, to permit full re-integration for the youngster's school career.

Our findings are less clear in terms of the choice of special program for youngsters with behaviour disorders. Prevailing philosophy in special education dictates that the least restrictive setting be considered first. For these youngsters, the least restrictive setting possible would appear to be a well-equipped resource room in a regular school. However, not enough research has been conducted on the capabilities of resource rooms to manage various problematic behaviours (see Figures 3.7 and 3.8). Pending more conclusive data, one might speculate that some pupils may display behaviours too disruptive to be managed in this type of setting. On the other hand, there are clear drawbacks to more self-contained special settings, especially as regards children's self-concept (see Figure 3.6). Perhaps the very fact of being removed to a special setting exacts a toll on self-concept. Program developers and evaluators might accept the challenge of determining if there are ways of delivering these programs while enhancing the participants' self-concepts. Educational planning would be greatly facilitated by more comprehensive research that would take into account the setting, the program, the teacher, and the behavioural profile of the individual pupil. In the meantime, it is imperative that each special program be carefully evaluated on an individual basis.

References

Byrd, B.T., Jr. (1975). The effects of three educational settings on achievement and self-concept of emotionally disturbed children (Doctoral dissertation, University of Michigan, 1974). **Dissertation Abstracts International, 35**, 7152A.

Calberg, C., and Kavale, K. (1980). The efficacy of special versus regular class placement for exceptional children: A meta-analysis. **Journal of Special Education, 14**, 295-309.

Calhoun, G., and Elliott, R.N. (1977). Self-concept and academic achievement of educable retarded and emotionally disturbed pupils. **Exceptional Children, 43**, 379-380.

Carpenter, R.L., and Apter, S.J. (1988). Research integration of cognitive-emotional inter ventions for behaviorally disordered children and youth. In M.C. Wang, M.C. Reynolds, and H.J. Walberg (Eds.), Handbook of special education: **Research and practice: Vol. 2. Mildly handicapped conditions** (pp. 155-169). Oxford, England: Pergamon Press.

Egelund, N. (1982). Efterundersogelse af heldagsskoleelever [A reexamination of students in the "All Day Long" School]. **Skolepsykologi, 19**, 216-232. (From PSYCLIT CD-ROM database, Accession No. 72-21404).

Gerke, R.E. (1976). The effects of mainstreaming on the self-concept and reading achievement of exceptional children at the elementary level (Doctoral dissertation, Lehigh University, 1975). **Dissertation Abstracts International, 36**, 7337A-7338A.

Gershman, J. (1976). A follow-up study of graduates of the perceptual and behavioral special classes. Toronto: Toronto Board of Education, Research Dept.

Glavin, J.P., Quay, H.C., Annesley, F.R., & Werry, J.S. (1971). An experimental resource room for behaviour problem children. **Exceptional Children, 38,** 131-137.

Gross, S. (1984). **Follow-up evaluation of Mark Twain students: Phase II.** Rockville, MD: Montgomery County Public Schools. (ERIC Document Reproduction Service No. ED. 256 801).

Gupta, Y. (1986). Observing the work of a tutorial unit. **British Journal of Special Education, 13,** 107-109.

Halpern, W.I., Kissel, S., & Gold, J. (1978). Day treatment as an aid to mainstreaming troubled children. **Community Mental Health Journal, 14,** 319-326.

Haring, N.G., and Phillips, E.L. (1966). **Educating emotionally disturbed children.** New York: McGraw-Hill.

Johnson, N., Cassie, J.R., and Hundert, J. (1986). Treating emotionally disturbed children: A question of cost-effectiveness. Unpublished manuscript, Brock University, St. Catharines.

Light, R.J. and Pillemer, D.B. (1984). **Summing up: The science of reviewing research.** Cambridge, MA: Harvard University Press.

McClure, G., and Ferguson, B. (in press). Predictors of children's school placements following psychiatric day treatment and special education programs. **Behavioral Disorders.**

McClure, G. (1990). Long-term follow-up data of behaviorally disordered children. Personal communication.

Nelson, C.M., and Rutherford, R.B., Jr. (1988). Behavioral interventions with behaviorally disordered students. In M.C. Wang, M.C. Reynods, & H.J. Walberg (Eds.), **Handbook of special education: Research and practice: Vol. 2. Mildly handicapped conditions** (pp. 125-153). Oxford, England: Pergamon Press.

O'Leary, S.G., and Schneider, M.R. (1977). Special class placement for conduct problem children. **Exceptional Children, 44,** 24-30.

Porter, W.R. (1977). A descriptive follow-up study of the initial population of a special public school (Doctoral dissertation, University of Maryland, 1976). From **Dissertation Abstracts International, 37,** 70797A.

Purdom, D. (1979, April). A public school comprehensive interdisciplinary day treatment program for preadolescents and adolescents with severe learning and behavioral disturbances. Paper presented at the Annual International Convention, The Council for Exceptional Children, Dallas, TX. (ERIC Document Reproduction Service No. ED 171 081).

Quay, H.C., Glavin, J.P., Annesley, F.R., & Werry, J.S. (1972). The modification of problem behaviour and academic achievement in a resource room. **Journal of School Psychology, 10,** 187-197.

Rosenthal, R. (1984). **Meta-analytic procedures for social research.** Beverly Hills, CA: Sage.

Rubin, E.Z., Simson, C.B., and Betwee, M.C. (1966). **Emotionally handicapped children and the elementary school.** Detroit: Wayne State University Press.

Sack, W., Mason, R., and Collins, R. (1987). A long-term follow-up study of a children's psychiatric day treatment center. **Child Psychiatry and Human Development, 18,** 58-68.

Safer, D.J., Heaton, R.C., and Parker, F.C. (1981). A behavioral program for disruptive junior high school students: Results and follow-up. **Journal of Abnormal Child Psychology, 9**, 483-494.

Schneider, B.H. (1982). Predictors of post-intervention community adjustment for emotionally disturbed elementary school students. **Journal of Clinical Child Psychology, 11**, 157-162.

Schneider, B.H. (1991). Reviewing previous research by meta-analysis. In B. Montgomery and S. Duck (Eds.), **Studying interpersonal interaction**. New York: Guilford.

Skiba, R., and Casey, A. (1985). Interventions for behaviourally disordered students: A quantitative review and methodological critique. **Behavioral Disorders, 10**, 239-252.

Slavin, R.E. (1987). Best-evidence synthesis: Why less is more. **Educational Researcher, 16**, 15-16.

Smith, C.R., Wood, F.H., and Grimes, J. (1988). Issues in the identification and placement of behaviorally disordered students. In M.C. Wang, M.C. Reynolds, and H.J. Walberg (Eds.), **Handbook of special education: Research and practice: Vol. 2. Mildly handicapped conditions** (pp. 95-123). Oxford, England: Pergamon Press.

Syropoulos, M. (1987). High School Development Center: **An alternative school for ninth and tenth grades**. Evaluation report, 1986-87. Detroit, MI: Detroit Public Schools, Dept. of Evaluation and Testing. (ERIC Document Reproduction Service No. ED 298 227).

Upshur, B. (1977). **Analysis of Satellite program for disruptive children**. Final report. Washington, DC: National Institute of Education, Career Education Program. (ERIC Document Reproduction Service No. ED 136 468).

Vacc, N.A. (1968). A study of emotionally disturbed children in regular and special classes. **Exceptional Children, 35**, 197-204.

Valero-Figueira, E. (1978). An exploration of the achievement, self-concept, and school morale of emotionally disturbed children in different special education settings (Doctoral dissertation, University of Michigan, 1978). **Dissertation Abstracts International, 39**, 3521A-3522A.

Weinstein, L. (1974). **Evaluation of a program for re-educating disturbed children: A follow-up comparison with untreated children**. Final report. Nashville, TN: George Peabody College for Teachers, John F. Kennedy Center for Research on Education and Human Development. (ERIC Document Reproduction Service No. ED 141 966).

Wood, F.H. (1990). Issues in the Education of Behaviorally Disordered Students. In M.C. Wang, M.C. Reynolds, and H.J. Walberg (Eds.), **Handbook of special education: Research and practice: Synthesis of Findings** (pp. 101-117). Oxford, England: Pergamon Press.

SECTION 4

PROVINCE-WIDE PERSPECTIVE ON PLACEMENT AND PROGRAMMING FOR BEHAVIOUR-DISORDERED PUPILS

ABSTRACT

The purpose of this section was to review the policies, placement practices, and plans for pupils identified as behaviour disordered. It is the result of contacts between the research team and teachers, administrators, and parents in selected jurisdictions throughout Ontario.

Separate focus groups of administrators, parents, and teachers were organized in each of 13 participating school boards. Teacher and administration groups in each board reacted to standard hypothetical case descriptions, indicating how their board would handle the pupil in question. This method facilitated comparison of practices across boards, despite the fact that the pupils that each designated as behaviourally exceptional might be quite dissimilar. All focus groups, including the parents' groups, participated in a semi-structured interview designed to elicit their perceptions. In the final stage of information gathering, telephone interviews were conducted between a senior administrator of each board and a consultant from the Faculty of Administration of the University of Ottawa.

The authors' conclusions suggest the need for a carefully planned sequential series of improvements in schools' ability to accommodate increasing behaviour problems. Long-term planning should feature preventive programming, but not be limited to it. Of special note is the recommendation that part of the action plan should involve careful reconsideration of the usefulness of identifying individual pupils as behaviourally exceptional.

This research indicates a marked need for standards for integrated programs that focus on the goals of the individual child's program, as well as on the overall quality of the classroom and school context.

The authors conclude by noting that training in behaviour management and in educating pupils whose social behaviour is problematic must become a more central feature of the training of teachers and other school personnel. It is suggested that the Ministry of Education renew its efforts to ensure that adequate mental health services are provided to children and families across the province, and that these services are well coordinated with other ministries and special services in the schools.

The legal status of special education programs in Ontario changed radically with the advent of mandated special education in 1985. In 1990, the Ministry of Education requested a review of policies, placement practices, and plans of selected school boards with regard to two groups of exceptional pupils studied in the present report. This section reviews policies and placement practices for one of these groups, namely, pupils identified as behaviour disordered. The results of contacts between the research team and teachers, administrators, and parents in selected jurisdictions throughout the province are presented. These contacts took place in late 1991 and early 1992.

Multiple data collection methods were utilized to probe current policies and practices in the boards selected, the perceptions of major stakeholders about the adequacy of current programs and procedures, and their opinions about future needs. With the cooperation of contact persons in each school board, separate focus groups of administrators, parents, and teachers were organized in each of the 13 participating boards. Teacher and administration groups in each board reacted to standard hypothetical case descriptions, indicating how their board would handle the pupil in question. This method facilitated comparison of practices across boards, despite the fact that the pupils each designate as behaviourally exceptional might be quite dissimilar. All focus groups – parents, administrators, and teachers – participated in a semi-structured interview designed to elicit their perceptions. In the final stage of information gathering, telephone interviews were conducted between a senior administrator of each school board and a consultant from the Faculty of Administration, University of Ottawa. This last step permitted corroboration of the impressions left by the focus group by an individual well versed in management but external to the special education field. It also provided an update on the views of the interviewees in light of the marked changes in the economic climate surrounding special education services during the year that elapsed from the beginning of data collection in early 1991 to the finalization of this report in November 1992.

Consistent with the case study approach specified by the Ministry, this report focuses on the perceptions of teachers, parents, and administrators and their reaction to material from case files. It does not feature the empirical evaluation of any program. However, the reader is referred to the previous section for a synthesis of evaluation research conducted in many jurisdictions, including Ontario.

Sampling Procedures

It was imperative that every attempt be made to generate an unbiased sample that would be reasonably representative of the province. Therefore, it was decided to engage an independent consultant with appropriate expertise, Dr. Rama Nair of the Department of Epidemiology and Community Medicine, University of Ottawa, to generate the sample. Boards were selected randomly within each of five large regions (South, East, West, North, and Metropolitan Toronto). In order to represent the distribution of pupil enrolment across the province as accurately as possible, census data was used to specify constraints on the selection of boards for the final sample. Accordingly, one separate and two public boards (one with large pupil enrolment, the other small) were selected within the Southern, Eastern, and Western regions. One public and one separate board were selected for both Metropolitan Toronto and the North. This resulted in the automatic selection of the Metropolitan Toronto Separate School Board, the only separate school board in its region. The automatic inclusion of this board, while a violation of the random sampling, enabled the participation of the parents and teachers of the large numbers of behaviour-disordered pupils served by this board. This procedure resulted in somewhat higher representation of the Northern region and of predominantly French-speaking boards than their proportion of provincial pupil enrolment. All contacts with the two boards where French was the primary language of instruction were conducted in that language. Table 4.1 is a schematic depiction of the final sample.

With the exception of Metro Separate, each initial selection was accompanied by two alternate boards in the same category. These were to be contacted in a pre-specified order if the first board selected declined to participate. It was necessary to contact the alternate boards in many of the regions.

Each board was permitted to decide which administrators would participate in the administrators' focus group. Local contact persons within each board helped derive a procedure for sampling potential participants for the focus groups of teachers and parents, taking into account geographical patterns within the catchment area as well as the board's organization

Table 4.1
Breakdown of School Boards in Ontario Focus Group Sample

	Separate	Public
North	1	1
South	1	2
Central	1	1
East	1	2
West	1	2

of special services. Teacher focus groups consisted of teachers who had experience with behaviour-disordered (BD) children in either regular classrooms or self-contained settings. In some large boards, the Research Department helped develop careful, elaborate sampling procedures for teacher and parent participants in focus groups. In some small boards, sampling was not necessary, since all potential participants could be accommodated. In other boards, sampling procedures were more informal.

Teacher and administrator focus groups typically involved 10 to 15 participants. In contrast, parent groups were usually smaller, though invitations had been extended to many more parents. One board decided not to permit a parent focus group. In one other board, no parents arrived. Parent participation was much lower than in the focus groups conducted in the same locations on different dates by this research team with parents of developmentally challenged pupils.

The full text of all focus group sessions was transcribed. Research assistants who were not involved as interviewers extracted the major themes and categorized the responses for the synthesis reported below.

Hypothetical Case Studies

Creation of Case Vignettes

The writing team consisted of a school social worker and a special education teacher. Both members had extensive experience with behaviour-disordered youngsters in schools. They were instructed to write descriptions of youngsters who might be referred to Identification, Placement, and Review Committees (IPRCs) because of behaviour problems. The case descriptions were to provide enough personal detail for them to be considered real. While features of cases from the team members' professional experiences were allowed, these were to be composites of various children, with identifying features carefully disguised. They were instructed to develop case descriptions for which the optimal special education placement would be debatable. The writing team developed six case vignettes, of which two were selected as best representing a range of ages, genders, and problem behaviours. The following are excerpts from the case descriptions.

The first case, named Jack, is an eight-year-old grade three student who had changed schools frequently, seven times since kindergarten. Jack has a quick temper and is frequently involved in fights at recess. In class, Jack is impulsive and defiant. All available assessments indicate that he is of average to above-average intelligence, though his written work is well below the norm. Jack and his younger sister are being raised by their father. They have infrequent contact with their mother.

Jenny, the second case, is 14 years old, and is repeating grade eight. She is repeating the grade because of chronic truancy. She is aloof and quiet at school and totally uninterested in schoolwork, though she seems able to get along with other pupils at times and seems to have no learning problems per se. She reports having a "nervous stomach", which medical examination was unable to confirm. The school is concerned that recommendations for outside counselling for Jenny are not being acted upon by her parents.

Method

Each case vignette was read to each focus group. After listening, the interviewer began with the following prompts. The participants were encouraged to elaborate on their responses. The interviewer queried responses with additional probes as necessary.

1. From the case description, where would this child most likely be placed within your school system?
2. In an ideal situation – where you could put together any program completely from scratch – what type of setting would you see as best for this child?
3. If money were no object, what setting would you see as best for this child?
4. If this child were older (younger), would your opinion as to the best placement be different?

Results

The consensus of about two-thirds of the focus groups was that Jack should remain in his regular grade three class with considerable supplementary support in both the academic and psychosocial domains, and that he would likely receive this placement within their setting. The minority opinion was for placement in a self-contained special class for pupils with behaviour disorders. There was no noticeable pattern of responses by geographical location, size of school board, or school support. These general positions were little different in an ideal situation where cost and history of service delivery were not a factor. However, most respondents indicated that they would prefer to see better resource support available to Jack and his regular class teacher. In one focus group, the best placement under current conditions was a self-contained class, but the respondents would have opted for regular class placement with support if the budget allowed for adequate resource help. Conversely, one other group stated that Jack should be placed in a regular class with support under current conditions, but that ideally they would like a self-contained class to be available for him.

Most groups felt that an older pupil with a similar behavioural profile would also be enrolled in a regular program. However, they emphasized the need for careful timetabling, taking into account the academic demands of each course and the personality of each teacher.

Focus groups were unanimous that Jenny should remain in her regular class with resource help and outside counselling. Teachers in one focus group mentioned that pupils like her are sometimes formally identified and placed in a self-contained setting, but that they themselves would not advocate it.

Conclusion

These results indicated general though not unanimous support for regular class placement with support for pupils presenting moderate behaviour problems. There was considerable concern that the support provided to pupils, families, and teachers be adequate. These impressions do not necessarily apply to cases of severe behaviour disorder.

Semi-Structured Focus Group Interviews

Method

Following the case vignettes, the interviewers asked a standard series of questions designed to elicit the participants' perceptions of the board's policies and procedures regarding behaviour-disordered pupils. The Appendix displays the standard interview prompts. Respondents were encouraged to introduce any issues they considered relevant to the major topics. The interviewers were instructed to probe as needed in order to understand the answers given to the pre-specified prompts and any additional issues that arose.

Results: Policies and Practices Regarding Identification Procedures

In several of the school board focus groups, teachers expressed profound concern about the escalating level of violence in the schools and about their own safety. Expressions of this growing alarm were most graphic in several of the teacher focus groups from urban boards, but were also very evident in the interview protocols of teacher focus groups in one of the northern boards and one of the most rural. Respondents believed not only that the level of problem behaviour had increased in recent years, but that there will be more behaviour problems in the future. Several of the boards had organized task forces to develop policy with regard to the handling of violent behaviour.

In contrast with their concern about these behaviours, most of the parents, teachers, and administrators were quite opposed to formal identification of pupils as behaviourally exceptional. While they expressed a wide variety of reservations about this process, their objections to current identification procedures were not voiced heatedly. This issue does not seem to be of high priority in comparison with the many concerns about programming and placement issues, which are discussed below. Teachers and parents alike believed that formal identification of youngsters as behaviour disordered leads more to stigma and social rejection than to any concrete improvement of the child's education and personal adjustment. The consensus seems to be that formal identification is sporadic in comparison to the number of pupils in actual need of service because of social, behavioural, and emotional difficulties. Some respondents indicated that many of these pupils are more likely to be identified as learning-disabled in order to avoid the stigma attached to being labelled as behaviour-disordered while still permitting special education assistance. Since behavioural exceptionalities are very often accompanied by, and perhaps linked to, learning disabilities and academic underachievement, this inexact approach to labelling is not seen as very problematic. A few of the parents interviewed were familiar with the support network available to the parents of gifted, learning-disabled, and developmentally challenged children. They felt that when other areas of exceptionality are identified, many avenues of support and information are opened. This rarely happens when a child is identified as behaviour disordered.

Teachers in some of the more isolated boards felt that formal identification was not productive unless facilities were available for corrective programming. In several boards, the teachers questioned the time spent in the IPRC process at the secondary level, where no special assistance was available for behaviour-disordered children. Local conditions in many boards influenced not only the de facto criteria for identification, but also the perceived results. Identification and programming are seen as difficult when students move frequently from board to board, where there are unpredicted increases in enrolment, and where unfavourable economic and social conditions are seen as exacerbating behaviour problems.

While somewhat disenchanted with current identification procedures, many parents and some teachers expressed a strong desire for early identification of problems, which would lead to preventive early intervention. There were numerous reports that younger children were being referred more frequently for behavioural support services, a practice that several boards planned to expand. There was also considerable enthusiasm for primary prevention efforts aimed at preventing behaviour problems before they arise.

Dissatisfaction with the identification process may relate to displeasure with the assessment procedures typically offered. While some teachers shared this concern, it was particularly vehement among parents, who rarely felt that they had obtained an understanding of their children's difficulties. Many parents felt that, while their children's problems were being summarily categorized as behaviour disorders, there were other underlying conditions as yet undiagnosed that played a major causal role. Some parents were curious as to how the schools differentiate between behaviourally exceptional pupils and other categories. Where a child was reported to have both behavioural and learning problems, many parents reported being told that the learning problems were due to emotional difficulties or poor self-concept. They felt that their children's academic progress was being sacrificed because schools saw it as a lesser priority.

Most parents felt that problems had been allowed to persist for far too long before they were informed of them, or before meaningful assessment and intervention were attempted. Some others felt that they were being deluged with constant telephone calls about incidents at school that, in their opinion, the schools should be handling. Some administrators and parents maintained that there was very good cooperation between parents and schools in all aspects of the identification-placement-review process. Others pointed out that there were wide discrepancies among parents in their willingness to become involved.

One principal expressed a need to differentiate between simple misbehaviour and problematic behaviour related to "something medical". Some teachers felt that assessments often failed to place adequate weight on classroom behaviour as a source of information. Some teachers perceived that withdrawn pupils, particularly passive female pupils, were receiving less attention than acting-out males.

Results: Policies and Practices Regarding Placement Procedures and Options

Virtually all the administrators interviewed espoused a philosophy of integration wherever possible. Teachers and administrators in several boards perceived pressure from the community to achieve complete integration. However, there appeared to be many discrepancies as to what this means and how this philosophy is implemented. There are discrepancies in placement options not only among boards, but also within boards and schools. Larger, urban boards tended to have a wider range of services for behaviour-disordered pupils, but even in large urban boards with many services available, teachers felt that, in actual practice, behaviour problems are handled very differently in different schools. In one large urban board, schools were permitted to take their own decision as to the degree of integration implemented. There was an even wider range of service provision in the smaller, more rural boards. Several of the smaller and more isolated boards had initiated task forces and pilot programs in order to better accommodate youngsters with behaviour disorders; more options exist for children located in schools where these pilot programs exist. Most of the parents were totally unaware of the boards' philosophies with regard to pupils with behaviour disorders.

Descriptions of the placement procedures followed in most boards were essentially enumerations of Ministry requirements. Some parents and most teachers reported that communication was better between home and school on a daily, informal basis than in connection with the IPRC. Most parents and some teachers and administrators felt that IPRC procedures had become so formalized that they were intimidating. Many parents were bewildered in this situation, and felt they did not have the knowledge to make the placement decisions being thrust upon them. Some parents felt that the IPRC procedures permitted only a cursory understanding of their children as a basis for decision making. A few teachers remarked that IPRC procedures were slow and cumbersome, and resulted in extensive paperwork.

There seemed to be considerable variation in the information used by IPRCs in taking decisions. Some teachers expressed the need for greater teacher input, advocating a system that would belong to the people who would use it most directly. Where there was a high degree of teacher input through an in-school review committee prior to an IPRC meeting, teachers seemed more accepting of the IPRC process. In general, teachers and administrators expressed fewer reservations about IPRC procedures than parents, and seemed to feel less strongly about them.

There was a consensus among administrators and teachers that their ability to provide for youngsters with behaviour disorders depended heavily on the availability of parallel mental health services for the children and their families. There were enormous fluctuations in the availability of such services, as well as in satisfaction with them and with the coordination of these services with educational programming. Some school personnel felt that community agencies failed to provide concrete, practical support to parents in need, such as, for example, child care workers to assist with problematic behaviour at home. There was some feeling that the roles of schools and community agencies were excessively blurred, with school personnel assuming a de facto role as mental health workers, and mental health workers making decisions about school programming. The rapid turnover of personnel providing mental health services in smaller communities has impeded liaison with schools in some areas.

Teachers and administrators were virtually unanimous in a strong conviction that family problems are the root of most behavioural exceptionalities, and that more and better services are needed for families. Therefore, some saw the school as playing only a "band-aid" role. They expressed resentment at the fact that sometimes services for families were unavailable, families refused to utilize them or discontinued their participation, and the schools could not get information about the family interventions conducted by outside agencies. Parents, in turn, expressed concern that educators blamed them for their children's behaviour problems. They often felt at a loss to explain or deal with their children's difficult behaviour. Several parents indicated the need for an ombudsperson to act as liaison with school boards and community agencies.

There was some concern that the prevailing philosophy of integration was not being well translated into allocation of resources, development of programs, and placement options. For example, teachers in one rural board spoke of a case for which a very costly array of professional and non-professional services would be available for a behaviour-disordered boy if he were removed from the community to a distant treatment centre, but absolutely no funds were available for even a teacher's aide if he were to be accommodated in his own school, which was willing to work with him. On the other hand, several administrators observed that youngsters placed in self-contained units seldom return to regular class settings. In a number of boards, programs were not available in secondary schools for behaviour-disordered pupils, and teachers were expected to handle situations on an individual basis as they arose. Many of the secondary school teachers expressed emphatic frustration at the lack of available provisions.

In many boards, efforts to increase the viability of integrated placements were underway. These included increased resource support to students participating in regular programs for a full school day, as well as partially self-contained programs for pupils who would otherwise not be attending a program within a regular school. Pilot programs inspired a considerable degree of optimism where they were being implemented, even in isolated areas. Anecdotal evidence of success was offered by the respondents, such as some students completing their OACs, and others remaining in school when they would otherwise have been on continual suspension,

Teachers and administrators in some boards described increased provision of support teachers, child care workers, teachers' aides, social workers, and psychologists. There was little uniformity in their availability and, concomitantly, wide variation in the degree to which integrated placement options were perceived as feasible and predictable. The training, professional status, and supervision of child care workers and teachers' aides varied enormously. Some boards provided initial training for teachers' aides, but not ongoing development. Many teachers observed that the success of behaviour-disordered students varied from classroom to classroom. They alluded to teachers whose personal style is particularly adept at dealing with behavioural problems, or whose classroom organizations were particularly suited to the demands of these children. Many teachers were eager to share a variety of ad hoc strategies they had developed to deal with problem behaviours. Some also described successful, informal team-teaching and resource-sharing arrangements within their schools. Several teacher focus groups expressed a desire for ongoing regular exchange of information about program practice. Several parent groups expressed a similar desire for a mutual support mechanism.

Some board participants reported very satisfactory in-school supervision arrangements that have worked well as an alternative to suspension. However, all teacher focus groups decried the marked inadequacies in their training in dealing with this type of pupil. Many expressed interest in receiving additional training, and felt that professional development (PD) workshops alone would not meet the need. A three-day summer seminar was organized by one of the urban boards, which also prepared a handbook and resource materials for its teachers. The board was pleased with the results.

In contrast with these reports of progress, some of the teacher focus groups were dissatisfied with communication within some schools. They felt that administrators must become more knowledgeable about the daily supports they saw as needed by teachers dealing with exceptional pupils in the regular classroom, and more committed to providing them.

Enthusiasm for integration stopped short when some of the focus groups began to concentrate on the needs of pupils whose behaviour constituted danger to others. Many parents and teachers wanted these children "out of the way", but had little clear idea as to what should be done for them. There was little confidence that self-contained classes could do much for this type of pupil. Suspension and home instruction appear to be in common use for extreme cases, with considerable variation in what is considered extreme.

Results: Policies and Practices Regarding Review of Pupil Progress

Most teachers and administrators felt that the mandated annual review of the student's placement and progress was a sound investment of time. In several boards, more frequent review procedures had been instituted, especially where the student's behaviour changed or where no progress was evident. Respondents emphasized that these annual reviews must feature as much involvement as possible of teachers and support personnel who know the student well and are directly involved in programming. In a few focus groups, teachers mentioned that review and accountability procedures for fully integrated behaviour-disordered pupils were in need of further refinement.

Several boards provided a multidisciplinary support team to consult on programming and review progress. Teachers and administrators expressed satisfaction with involving the team in major decisions.

Transition years were seen as particularly problematic for behaviourally exceptional pupils and their teachers. One board was pleased with the results of more intensive contact between the elementary and secondary panels regarding pupils about to transfer.

Telephone Interview Regarding Policy Development

Method

The telephone interviews focused on the development of policy. Each participating school board was reached by telephone and asked for the superintendent responsible for special education, or a substitute as necessary. Each participant was asked the following questions:
1. Does your position make you knowledgeable about board policy and resource use for behaviourally disordered children?
2. Does your board offer segregated or integrated programs for these children? How has the board determined this policy?
3. Do policies exist that describe criteria for student admission and staffing?
4. Are policies in place that prescribe the allocation of resources to these programs?
5. Do these policies drive resource use? Please describe how this works. Are trustees involved at this level?
6. What effect will economic constraints have on these programs?

The interviews lasted on average thirty minutes; some were longer. Detailed notes were made. A matrix was developed to give a cross-sectional depiction of the links between policy and the allocation of resources across the province. Additional questions were asked as needed.

Results

The responses to the first few questions indicated that appropriate persons familiar with the boards' policies had been located. All subjects interviewed acknowledged that they were able to describe the policies and resource decisions affecting these programs. Special education advisory committees were seen most frequently as the source of the boards' policies on programming for behaviour-disordered pupils. These committees are composed of advocates for the children and their parents. They were seen as very active in stimulating new programs, but very prone to underemphasizing cost issues.

Common standards for the operation of special programs for behaviour-disordered pupils do not appear to exist either in the research literature or across school boards in Ontario. A number of respondents expressed the need for standards of quality control. Several participants suggested that the provincial government should be responsible for the development of such standards as an extension of existing legislation. Participants commented that provincial policy from the Ministry of Education did allow for differences in interpretation. Such flexibility was considered necessary in the implementation of directives regarding standards for programs.

A common theme was that economic constraint could cause a reduction in the resources allocated to the development of new models for service delivery. It was noted that, while there were some Ministry regulations about the provision of special programs, there were none governing their reduction when available financial resources become depleted. Several respondents felt that integrated programs would be in particular jeopardy because of the structures of existing collective agreements. Teachers' aides, who participate widely in integrated programs, could be the first to be eliminated. Some of the superintendents also anticipated that the positions of consultants would be sharply curtailed. Several respondents, particulary in the separate boards, indicated that the first cuts would likely affect the purchase of special equipment such as computers, as well as building repair and maintenance, before in-class personnel are reduced.

These impending changes were seen as generating fury on the part of parents, who are increasingly demanding better environments for their exceptional children. The consensus of these interviews was that "dollars will drive policy" notwithstanding Ministry directives for children with special educational needs. Viewing every child as an individual with individual needs was seen as a policy that is no longer viable once resources are not available to meet the identified needs.

General Conclusions

1. As detailed above, the identification of individual pupils as behaviourally exceptional does not appear consistent with the needs of many pupils who exhibit problematic behaviour at school and with the needs of their families. If the needs of this group alone are considered, an identification procedure that would categorize the services needed, rather than the pupil, would appear to be an improvement. This observation does not necessarily apply to other areas of exceptionality that were not considered in this research, such as youngsters with learning disabilities, for example. Most exceptional pupils in other categories probably derive more benefit from being formally identified than behaviourally exceptional pupils.

2. There is wide diversity among schools in tolerance thresholds for problem behaviour and in the level they consider as warranting formal identification. To the degree that these disparities represent different local values, they are not necessarily objectionable. However, these differences could also reflect unequal access to the resources needed for special programming. In that case, and if current procedures for identification of pupils as behaviourally exceptional are to remain, clearer guidelines may be needed as to when identification should take place and what type of assessment should be conducted prior to identification of a pupil.

Table 4.2
Major Themes Raised in the Focus Groups

Issues Raised — Behaviour Disordered	Administrators	Teachers	Parents
Academic and Behavioural Problems Connected		X	
Age Differences in Needs for Service	X	X	
Assessment/Diagnosis – Practices	X	X	X
Availability of Services/Programs	X	X	X
Classroom Environment, Effects on Pupil Behaviour	X	X	X
Concern for Dropouts	X	X	
Concern re: Local Conditions	X		
Concern re: Violence in Schools		X	
Degree of Integration – Policy/Practice	X	X	X
Discipline/Suspension/Expulsion	X	X	
Early Identification		X	X
Equipment Needs	X	X	
Etiology of Behaviour Disorders	X		X
Expectations, Parents	X		X
Expectations, Teachers	X	X	
Families, Need for Counselling	X		
Familiy as Cause of Behaviour Problem	X	X	
Increase in Behaviour Problems Over Time	X	X	
IPRC – Time/Composition		X	
IPRC – Usefulness	X	X	X
Ministry of Education – Role	X	X	
Ministry of the Child, One Ministry for Children's Services	X	X	
Morale, Emotional Tone, Optimism	X	X	X

Issues Raised — Behaviour Disordered (cont'd)	Administrators	Teachers	Parents
More Effective Annual Review of Pupil Progress	X	X	X
Need for Crisis Intervention Team		X	
Parent Involvement/School Communication	X	X	X
Philosophy — Articulation	X	X	X
Placement Decisions, Responsibilities	X	X	X
Prevention Practices	X	X	
Programs — Delivery & Evaluation	X	X	X
Questions re: Teacher's Role	X	X	X
Relevance of Cost Factors	X	X	X
Residential or Day Treatment, COMSOC Facilities, Section 27	X	X	
Resource / Withdrawal Programs	X	X	
Services of Treatment Facilities / Agencies	X	X	X
Social Skills Training for Pupils	X	X	
Staffing, Child Care Workers		X	
Staffing, Psychologists, Psychiatrists, Social Workers, Counsellors	X	X	X
Staffing, Teachers/Teacher's Aides	X	X	X
Stigma, Ostracism, Social Rejection, Labeling	X	X	X
Support Team, In-School Team, Professional Back-Up	X	X	
Teachers – Preparation Time		X	
Training – Administrators	X	X	
Training, In-Service	X	X	X
Training, Pre-Service	X	X	
Transitions, Elementary/Secondary/Community	X	X	

3. Problematic aggression was addressed by most of the respondents; there was little mention of youngsters with internalizing disorders. While problematic aggression is more stable than problematic social withdrawal (Parker and Asher, 1987), there is a danger that the widespread concern about aggressive behaviour will lead to total inattention to depressed pupils. This latter group may not be well served by being added to programs conceived essentially for aggressive youngsters. At the very least, Ministry documents should include these needs, which could be communicated more extensively to teachers as part of their in-service training.

4. Teachers, administrative officers, and parents identified a need for ombudspersons or liaison persons to facilitate communication among families, teachers, boards, and outside agencies. These parents should be available to coordinate information, facilitate communication, and advise regarding unfulfilled needs for service. Some communities have established coordinating committees to deal with very difficult cases in need of service. However, it should not be necessary for services to break down or for the pupil to be identified as "hard to serve" in order to access the liaison person. Hopefully, such liaison persons could help deal with any breakdowns in communication and service delivery at a very early stage. In order to accomplish this, they must be clearly identified to parents.

5. Parents need better information in order to take the decisions mandated to them. They should have an opportunity to visit a proposed placement. It is doubtful that they would be denied this opportunity in any of the school boards in the current sample. However, many of the parents interviewed found the placement process highly intimidating and would not be likely to request a visit if it were not offered. Equipping parents with other data useful in their decision making would enhance their involvement in the process, and might reduce their reliance on hearsay. Therefore, where a change in placement is contemplated, parents should be provided with a clear profile of the new environment. Ideally, the board's own evaluation of the setting should be made available. If this is not possible, other indicators could be supplied, for example, the staff-student ratio, qualifications of the staff in dealing with this population, number of years the program has existed, average length of pupil enrolment (and range), some indication of outcome (e.g., how many pupils no longer need resource help, how many return to regular class), philosophy of the setting and specific behaviour management procedures used, how parents are involved, and what communication they can expect.

6. Current procedures mandate placement decisions based entirely on the needs of the individual pupil and parents' wishes. As indicated above (#1), the identification of individual pupils as behaviour disordered may not always be beneficial for them. However, given the widespread concern about escalating levels of violence in the schools by many of the participants in this study, the needs of the rest of the school community may have to be taken into account as well. Where a child's behaviour constitutes a physical danger to others, the needs of teachers and other pupils should be considered in reaching placement decisions. While this is probably happening already, formal recognition of this dimension appears to be important to the teacher participants in this study.

7. There are wide discrepancies between and even within boards in the proportions of pupils served in various types of settings. As noted earlier in this report, Ontario appears to permit greater local autonomy in models of service delivery than most other jurisdictions. This relates only partially to geographic factors and population served. The discrepancies among board policies did not correspond to any identifiable geographic or demographic pattern. It might be unwise to attempt to standardize the way in which services are delivered across Ontario beyond the Ministry's position that integrated services should be available to the

extent feasible and in accordance with parents' wishes. This position does not seem inconsistent with the general philosophies of most of the focus groups, who were more concerned with the way integration is being implemented. However, it is important to establish quality control standards for programming that could apply across settings. Specification of detailed standards is beyond the scope of this report. However, these might include:
   I. comprehensive multidisciplinary assessment, including evaluation of possible related causes such as learning problems;
   II. suitable staff training, including the opportunity for the staff to consult with well-trained professionals regarding both individual cases and the planning of the total classroom environment;
   III. clear classroom management procedures developed proactively to reduce problem behaviour and deal with it in a positive and proportional way when it occurs; and
   IV. provision for supervision of disruptive pupils as necessary in corridors, at recess, and in regular classes where they are integrated.

Obviously, there are costs involved in implementing programs to meet such quality standards. There appears to be general consensus of the focus groups that adequate integrated programs cannot be implemented without allocation of suitable resources, which is often not occurring. Even at a time of economic restraint, the needs of behaviourally exceptional pupils and the public's concern about not meeting them justify the investment.

8. Since dealing with problematic pupil behaviour is increasing and becoming a more integral part of the responsibilities of every teacher, it is imperative that teacher training include skills in this area. Pre-service training for all teachers must feature a more adequate introduction both to the needs of the behaviourally exceptional pupil and to effective programming within the regular classroom. Enhanced in-service training is also needed; this might include PD day workshops, but should also include opportunities for more intensive training as feasible and appropriate. Professional development should be more than reaction to a crisis. It must be implemented dynamically and systematically, evaluated continuously, and revised as necessary.

9. Successful programming in many cases depends on teamwork between teachers and child care workers or teachers' aides. It is important that these support personnel be given adequate training and supervision.

10. Many parents and teachers used the focus groups to trade blame for children's behaviour problems. It is important that Ministry documents emphasize the multiple aetiologies of children's behaviour disorders, recognizing that family factors are very important, but that schools can nonetheless have a positive impact (e.g., Rutter, Maugham, Mortimore, Ouston, and Smith, 1979). The success of the current thrust to provide suitable educational programming to behaviour-disordered pupils in their home schools depends partially on a parallel increase in the provision of mental health services to children in their homes and communities. Better liaison between school and mental health services may be facilitated by provision of community mental health services by Ministry of Community and Social Services (COMSOC) agencies within school facilities. Efforts might be made to sensitize community agencies to the service needs of children and families who do not meet criteria they set for service, or who still display problematic behaviours after intervention has terminated. In many communities, this may require community agencies to offer a more varied range of services to families, children, and schools. Direct support for parents unable to manage their children's behaviour, including parent relief as needed in exceptional cases, appears to be an urgent priority that should be brought to the attention of the appropriate agencies. While communication between school and community

agencies must be improved, it may be important for teachers and agency workers to delineate what type of information is important to share and likely to lead to educational benefit. There also seems to be a need for increased awareness of mandated requirements for the confidentiality of family information.

11. Identification and services must be provided across all grade levels, with no break in continuity during transition years or in secondary school. In some boards, program options in secondary schools did not seem flexible enough to accommodate pupils with exceptional behavioural problems. Whether there is formal or informal identification, behaviour-disordered pupils are present in high school classrooms. Development of new program options at the secondary level should receive high priority.

12. Many smaller and remote boards may not have the resources to provide adequately for youngsters with behavioural exceptionalities, particularly where extreme cases occur infrequently. Services in French and in the North are also limited. Consortia of several boards might consider establishing a shared, peripatetic resource team of specialists trained in diagnosing behavioural exceptionalities and related learning problems, prescribing programming in this area, and reviewing progress on a regular basis. It might be beneficial for some boards to purchase occasional services as needed from this team if their enrolments do not justify full-time specialized personnel. The team could also provide input on the design of new programs and the evaluation of existing ones. It should be noted that several such initiatives have already been undertaken in Northern Ontario. However, these teams have been primarily active in the identification and diagnosis of special needs at the level of the individual pupil, rather than in the development of programs.

13. As noted in our review of research submitted previously, evaluations of special programs for behavioural exceptionalities have yielded somewhat equivocal results. However, as discussed in that document, research to date has not adequately taken into account the quality of the programs evaluated. A demonstration centre that featured carefully selected and intensively trained staff supported by the best consultation available might be able to illustrate how effective an optimal program could be. Such a centre might be operated by a consortium of large boards or by the Ministry. It could also serve as a resource for teachers and professionals interested in improving programming for this population. Such a centre should not serve pupils from all over the province in any one location, which would be tantamount to establishing a new training school. Instead, it could take the form of specially enriched programming within a small number of schools, which would change every few years. Personnel could be seconded from boards, universities, and treatment centres as needed.

14. Decisions about the management of problem behaviour are very complex and often controversial. Most authorities advocate the involvement of a multidisciplinary team in these decisions; this was also endorsed by several of the focus groups. Therefore, Ministry documents might suggest a team format for decisions involving behaviour-disordered pupils. For the most part, this report has not advocated standardization of practice across the province. However, clearer Ministry guidelines regarding the use of suspension and alternatives to it might be helpful.

15. Schools have an important part to play in the development of programs for the primary and secondary prevention of behaviour disorder. Many such programs have been developed in conjunction with hospitals, clinics, and universities. It has been argued quite convincingly that schools are usually the most logical site for their implementation (Weissberg and Allen, 1986).

Concluding Summary

The general picture conveyed by the participants in this study was one of concern about behaviour problems in the schools. This concern was quite general across the province. Though there were some local differences, the overriding issues and problems seemed remarkably similar in urban and rural areas, in various regions of the province, and in English- and French-speaking boards.

To respond to the general province-wide alarm about increasing behaviour problems in the schools, a carefully planned sequential series of improvements is needed in schools' ability to accommodate these difficulties. Long-term planning should feature preventive programming, but not be limited to it. Part of the action plan should involve careful reconsideration of the usefulness of identifying individual pupils as behaviourally exceptional. If this practice is to remain, directives about its implementation would seem to be needed.

While most of the individuals interviewed across the province have little quarrel with the concept of serving as many pupils as possible in integrated settings, there is a marked need for standards for these integrated programs. Such standards must focus not only on the goals of the individual child's program, but on the overall quality of the classroom and school context. Inevitably, this will require more consistent allocation of resources to behaviour-disordered pupils in integrated settings. In the absence of adequate cost estimates, there is no reason to believe that the costs of a high-calibre integrated program are as high as those of self-contained classes or school operations within treatment settings. However, integrated behaviour-disordered pupils and their teachers require more support than they often receive at present.

Training in behaviour management and in educating pupils whose social behaviour is problematic must become a more central feature of the training of teachers and other school personnel. This does not mean that teachers and other school personnel should assume the roles of mental health professionals in dealing with behavioural, emotional, and family problems. In its contacts with other ministries, the Ministry of Education should redouble its efforts to ensure that adequate mental health services are provided to children and families across the province, and that these services are well coordinated with special services in the schools.

References

Parker, J., and Asher, S. (1987). Peer relations and later personal adjustment: Are low accepted children at risk? **Psychological Bulletin, 102,** 357-389.

Rutter, M., Maugham, B., Mortimore, P., Ouston, J., and Smith, A. (1979). **Fifteen thousand hours**. Cambridge: Harvard University Press.

Weissberg, R., and Allen, J. (1986). Promoting children's social skills and adaptive behaviour. In B.A. Edelstein and L. Michelson (Eds.), **Handbook of prevention** (pp. 153-175). New York: Plenum.

SECTION 5

EDUCATIONAL ENVIRONMENTS FOR THE DEVELOPMENTALLY CHALLENGED PUPIL: A "BEST EVIDENCE" RESEARCH SYNTHESIS

ABSTRACT

The nature of the optimal educational environment for pupils with developmental challenges is a matter of considerable controversy. This report is a quantitative summary of research in which various special education settings — regular class, resource room, special class, special school, and others are compared in terms of their impact on the functioning of these youngsters.

There are many limitations in reviewing this literature and in comparing the 10 studies. These are fully explored and discussed within the report. The review acknowledged that the objective of the researchers was to be based on the "best evidence" of the best designed studies only.

The results of each study are explored in terms of overall setting effects, publication bias, sampling procedure, age effects, and program effects separated by area of development (e.g., cognitive, motor, social/behavioural). In each of the 10 studies sampled, most of the effects favoured the more integrated setting.

This very clear conclusion must be tempered because of the two limitations of the data base. First of all, very few studies have featured random assignment of subjects to programs. Secondly, most of the studies compared semi-integrated options (e.g., special classes in regular schools) with special school settings. There are relatively few data available regarding the regular class placement of pupils with moderate developmental challenges.

Recent years have seen considerable changes in the educational experiences offered to developmentally handicapped individuals. Advances in theory and practice have been spurred by research findings that raise considerable doubt about the benefits of special classes and schools. Much of this educational research has focused on children with mild, rather than moderate or severe handicaps (e.g., Calberg and Kavale, 1980; Goldstein, Moss and Jordan, 1966). The purpose of this review is to synthesize research in which educational settings (regular class, regular school, special class, special school) are compared in terms of their impact on the development and progress of developmentally challenged pupils, previously referred to as "trainable" in many educational settings. Parents and professionals working with this population are frequently involved in decisions regarding the best educational setting for an individual child. This report examines the research basis for these decisions. In order to make this report accessible to teachers and others without extensive background in statistics and meta-analytic methods, the first section is devoted to a discussion of the difficulties inherent in reviewing research of this type and an explanation of the purposes and techniques of quantitative reviews of research.

Challenges in Reviewing This Literature

In addition to the general considerations discussed in Section 3, there are certain specific challenges in reviewing this group of studies. One of these is the lack of suitable control groups. In theory, it would be desirable to compare children who received one type of special programming with an equivalent, randomly assigned group who received another form of assistance, given the fact that it would be unethical to provide no help to pupils in need. However, this is rarely possible. Placement decisions are usually made by parents, teachers, and professionals based on their perceptions of where the individual pupil would be best placed (this is legally mandated in many jurisdictions, including the United States and Ontario). Therefore, many studies do not and cannot utilize fully comparable control groups. While they might compare the pupils' progress in one setting with pupils in another, these pupils may have exceptionalities that vary enormously in nature and severity, rendering comparison of the two groups highly problematic.

This is exacerbated by the fact that the subjects are rarely well described in these studies. The terms "trainable", "developmental challenge", and "moderate mental retardation" are not used uniformly across jurisdictions. Therefore, studies that at first appear comparable are often quite different in terms of the actual behavioural characteristics and functioning levels of the participants. Furthermore, the population of developmentally challenged youngsters in any setting is likely to be very heterogeneous in many ways. Group results, therefore, will indicate a program's success with the "average" pupil participant, obscuring a host of important differences among sub-groups and individuals.

Furthermore, very few studies have explored the interactions of setting, program, and teacher effects. For example, a study in which special schools were compared with special classes in regular schools would likely not differentiate among schools that provided a high degree of systematic language training or life skills preparation (not to mention how well these programs were implemented), nor between programs staffed by highly trained teachers and those staffed by teachers with less background. Therefore, the results of the study might not optimally portray the true potential of either type of program. In the absence of research in which setting, program, and teacher effects are comprehensively investigated, the following review focuses on studies in which different settings or placement options are compared.

Finally, introduction of certain traditional meta-analytic techniques may be highly problematic in this context. In many classic meta-analytic reviews, effect sizes are derived based on the pre-treatment to post-treatment within-group gain scores of each experimental or control group. If applied to the current review, this would lead to combining results of individuals that are too heterogeneous, as discussed above. As well, it may be inappropriate to interpret the magnitude of such change scores as discussed in standard texts. Use of such referents based on the distribution of the general population could underestimate the true importance of relatively small gains in cognitive, language, or motor functioning for this population. For these reasons, this review has been based on statistical between-group comparisons of each "treatment" group with its own "control" group — for example, a comparison of a program delivered in a separate school facility with a special class in a regular school in the same jurisdiction.

Method

A "Best Evidence" Synthesis

As mentioned above, not all studies on a given topic are of equal quality and usefulness. Our initial scan of the literature suggested that, in contrast with several well-designed studies, results of others are virtually impossible to interpret because: (1) subjects are so poorly described that it is impossible to characterize them under the general rubric of moderate mental retardation; (2) program descriptions are so sketchy that they cannot even be characterized in the most general terms (such as regular class, special class, etc.); (3) outcome measures are highly subjective (e.g., "40% were greatly improved according to the teacher who administered the program"); or (4) there is no comparison group at all.

Our first decision, then, was that our review would be based on the "best evidence" (Slavin, 1987) available; that is, the results of the best designed studies only, in contrast with the vast number of studies available that provide data of lesser value. As an alternative to the indiscriminate inclusion of all studies regardless of quality in a meta-analysis, Slavin proposed using only the studies of highest internal and external validity, according to pre-specified and justified inclusion criteria.

Meta-Analytic Synthesis of Comparisons Between Groups

Two types of data are useful in evaluating the changes in pupil behaviour and achievement that ensue from any program, treatment, or placement. The first is within-groups change, e.g., changes in pupil scores after participation in a program; the second is between-groups comparison. Most meta-analyses have focused exclusively on the first type of data. They have typically calculated an effect size for each experimental group in each study, as well as an effect size for each control group in each study. The mean effect size for the experimental groups is then compared with the corresponding statistic for the control groups. As discussed above, combining and averaging the effect sizes for the highly heterogeneous groups in the current data base would be highly problematic.

For these reasons, the second meta-analytic strategy was used in this study, consisting of a meta-analytic synthesis of between-groups comparisons. This has the advantage of maintaining the distinctness of each study to a greater degree than in traditional meta-analysis, permitting each experimental group to be compared with its own control group, whose subjects should be most comparable. Readers interested in comparing the results of this review with other quantitative literature reviews must bear this fundamental difference in mind.

Literature Search and Inclusion Rules

Thorough computer searches were conducted of the following data bases: Psychological Abstracts, ERIC documents, and Dissertation Abstracts International. However, we recognized that relevant articles might be overlooked by this procedure, because of the above-mentioned confusion in the terminology used to describe subjects. Therefore, once a relevant document was found, its bibliography was scanned for other relevant references. While several hundred interesting articles were located, most of these were program descriptions or theoretical discussions without any evaluative data.

In order to present conclusions based on the "best evidence" available (see above), the following criteria were set for studies to be included in the final sample:

1. The study (or an identifiable portion) had to be conducted with subjects described as moderately mentally retarded, trainable mentally retarded, or moderately developmentally handicapped in one of the following settings: regular class, special class, special school, treatment centre, or hospital. If a study involved more than one identifiable population (e.g., moderately retarded and aphasic), it was included only if specific sub-analyses were reported for the moderately retarded sample.
2. The study had to compare changes in these youngsters with those of a population of moderately retarded youngsters in a second type of setting; the control or comparison group had to be similar in age.
3. The study had to report changes in the participants' cognitive, language, or motor development, or adaptive behaviour, in a quantified manner suitable for meta-analysis.

Coding of Studies

Each study was independently coded by two research assistants with bachelor's degrees in psychology. They coded a total of 11 categories: diagnostic description of subjects, sample size, age, IQ, sex distribution, type of control group, method of assigning subjects to groups, source of outcome data (e.g., pupil, teacher, direct observation), dependent variable, teacher experience, and teacher strategy or treatment technique used. The two latter categories were dropped because of insufficient data. The two raters agreed exactly on 91 per cent of the individual coding decisions, and no coding category had inter-rater agreement of less than 80 per cent.

Results

Overview

A graphic presentation has been used to facilitate readability. In each of the graphs on the following pages, the effect-size estimate for each study (or each setting comparison in studies that involved three or more types of setting) is assigned a bar on a histogram. Please note that an effect-size estimate known as r (Rosenthal, 1984) was used in this study. There are several other types of effect-size statistics (delta, d, g, etc.). Therefore, the magnitudes of the effect cannot be compared with effect sizes from other meta-analyses if these have used other effect-size estimate statistics (however, these can be easily transformed).

Given the small number of effects and their heterogeneity, average effect sizes were not computed. Each bar represents the comparison between change estimates for two settings, as discussed above. For example, the first bar at the left in Figure 5.1 describes a comparison between changes of moderately retarded pupils in regular classes and special classes. Where the more restrictive setting (in this case, it could have been the special classes) has the higher effect size, the bar is drawn above the dividing line. However, since there are no studies in which there was a global effect size in favour of a more restricted setting, all bars in Figure 5.1 are drawn above the line (however, see Figure 5.6, where two of the eight bars are drawn below the line, since two of the eight studies indicated greater progress for the youngsters in more restricted settings on measures of adaptive behaviour). It is necessary to consult the legend to determine exactly which settings are being compared. The unshaded bar for the Beuter study indicates that it was a comparison between regular and special classes. It is important to remember that, while the results favoured the regular classes, this does not necessarily mean that the youngsters in the special class deteriorated; it might only mean that they did not make as much gain.

Overall Setting Effects

Figure 5.1 depicts overall findings, collapsed across age groups and dependent measures (adaptive behaviour; cognitive, language, or motor development). As shown, all overall effect sizes (i.e., collapsed across different types of outcome measures) favoured the less restrictive settings. However, there was considerable heterogeneity in the effects, ranging from extremely large to only slightly different from zero.

Sampling Procedures

In Figure 5.2, studies are separated by method used for assigning subjects to groups. The Toomey (1978) study merits particular attention because the subjects were randomly assigned to special classes and treatment centre, despite the obstacles discussed above. The two remaining portions of the graph compare other studies in which subjects could not

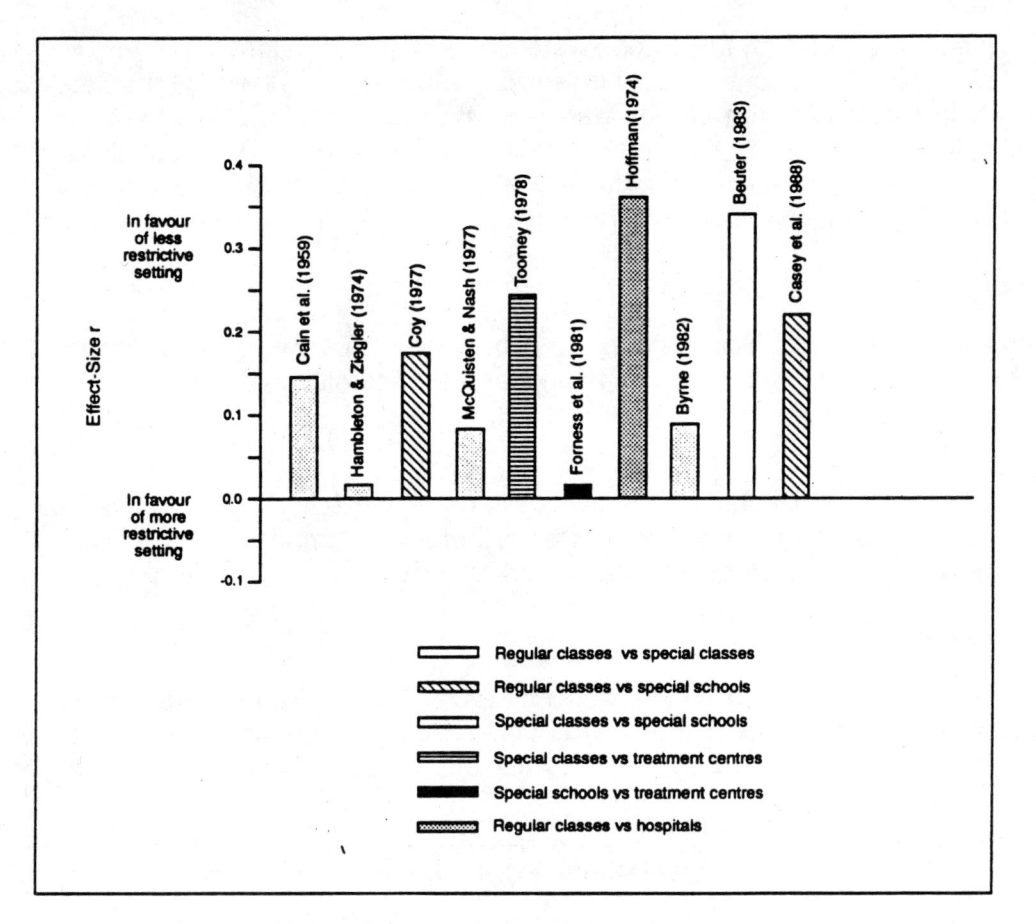

Figure 5.1 Effect Size by Setting

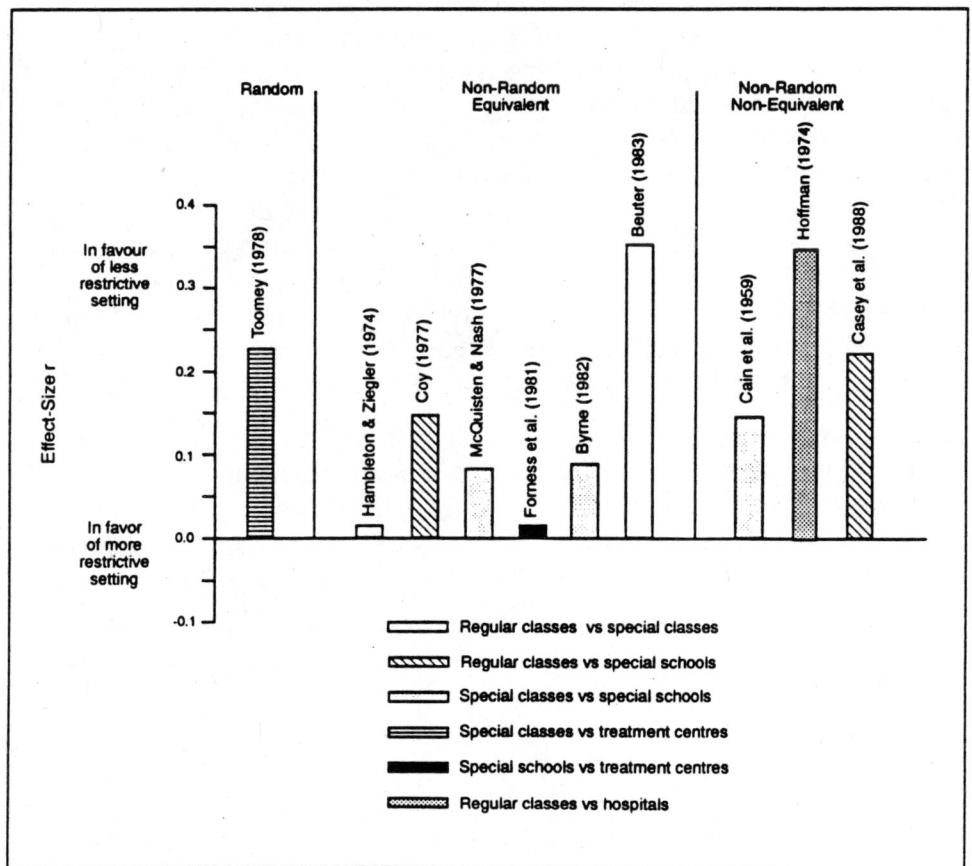

Figure 5.2 Effect Size by Sampling Procedure

be randomly assigned. In six studies, the groups were found to be equivalent at pre-test on the measures used. These seem to have slightly smaller effects on the average than the three studies in which the comparison groups were known to be non-equivalent from the start. The results of these three cannot be interpreted with great confidence, since the higher effect size for the less restricted setting may very well be attributed to the fact that the subjects were functioning at a higher level to begin with.

Publication Status

In Figure 5.3, studies are separated according to the publication status (i.e., journal, unpublished report, or thesis). No salient differences among these is discernible.

Age Effects

In Figure 5.4, effect sizes are separated by the average age of subjects. While no overall trend is discernible, it is noted that the studies that reported the smallest effects were among the five with average subject ages between 8 and 12 years.

Areas of Development

In Figures 5.5 through 5.8, results are broken down by area of development. As shown, there is little consistent deviation from the overall composite findings reported above. However, there are marked inconsistencies among the effect sizes within each area of development.

Conclusions

We believe that these studies constitute the "best evidence" available, although their many limitations, discussed above, indicate that they should be interpreted with caution. Nevertheless, there are some clear implications. The first is that the regular school option for moderately retarded is consistently supported by research; few findings in special education program evaluation are as unambiguous. While the results yield a clear indication of the comparability of these two settings, more restricted and less restricted, in current practice, they cannot determine whether the potential of any particular setting to implement an ideal program has been realized. However, because of the researchers' failure to differentiate among pupils' behavioural profiles or functioning levels, there might still be important individual differences in suitability for regular class placement. The fact that none of the comparisons involving regular class placement was based on random assignment of subjects exacerbates this. Therefore, further research in this area is sorely needed.

The second implication is the impossibility of determining from the original data sources whether the departures from the general pattern of findings are attributable to differences in subject characteristics, differences in program characteristics, or other factors. Therefore, it is imperative that each program as well as each child's progress be systematically evaluated. Hopefully, new research will consider the combined effects of setting, subject characteristics, and program.

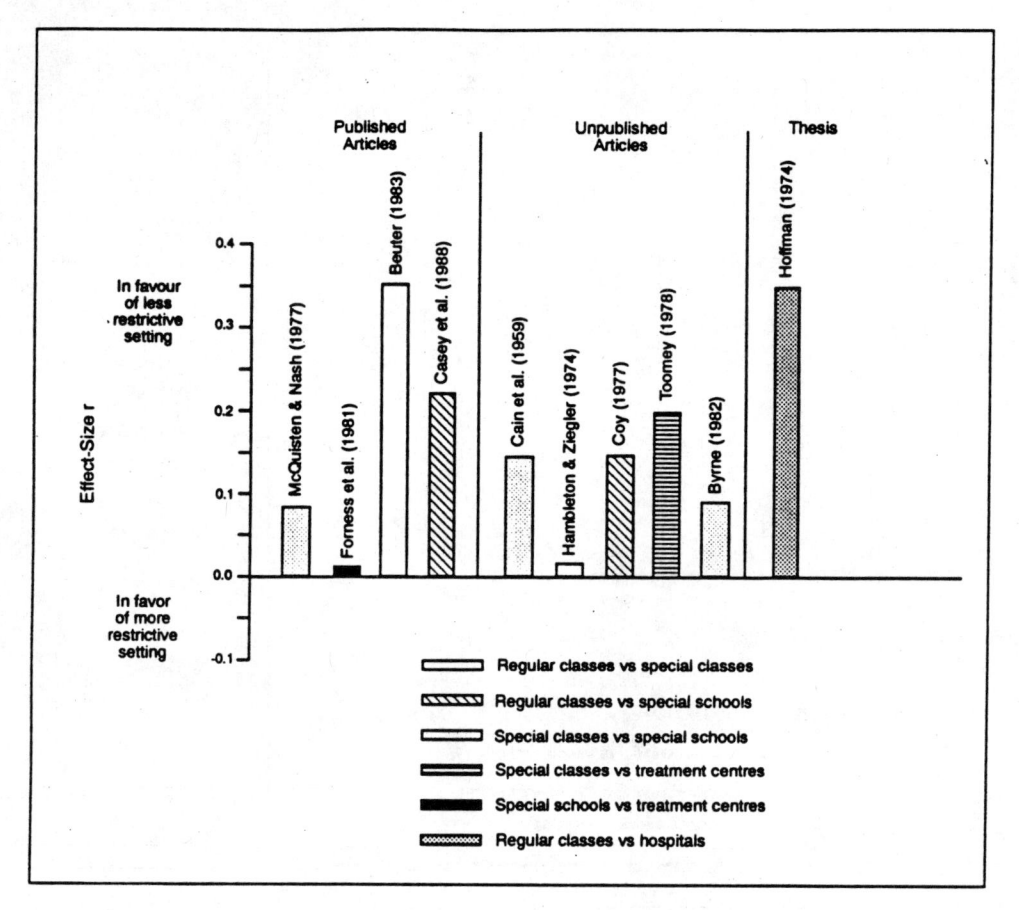

Figure 5.3 Effect Size by Publication Status

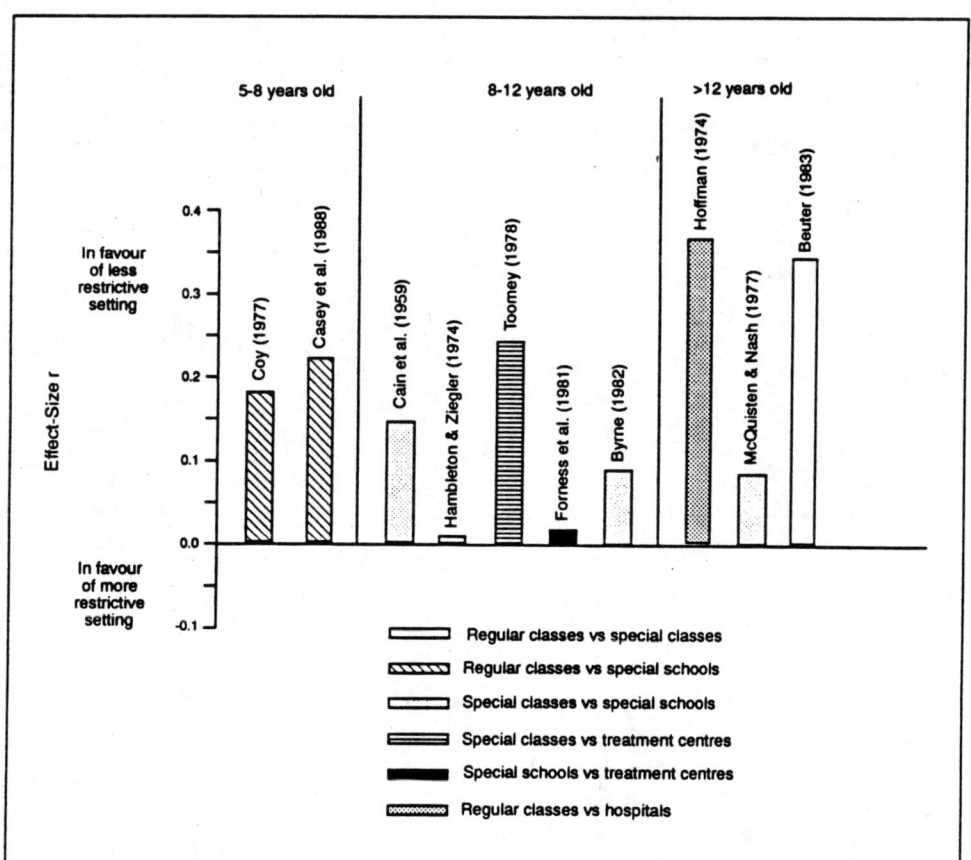

Figure 5.4 Effect Size by Mean Age

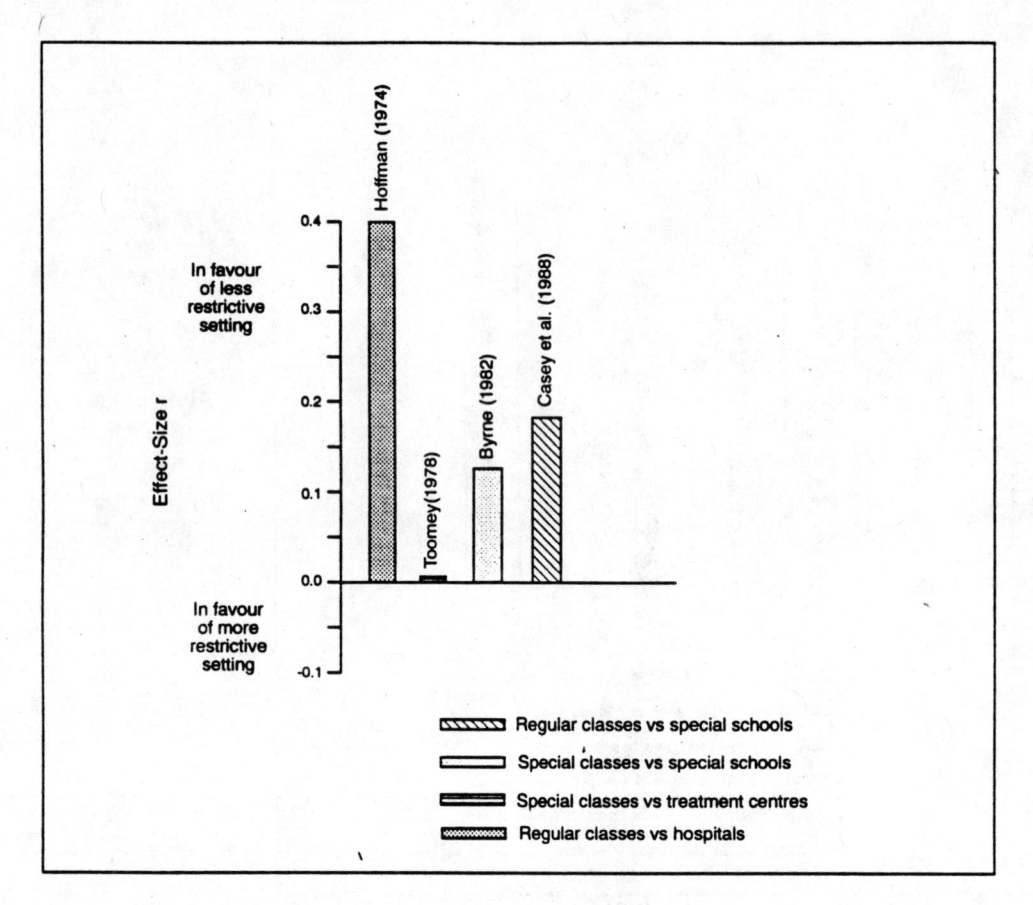

Figure 5.5 Effect Sizes for Language Development Measures

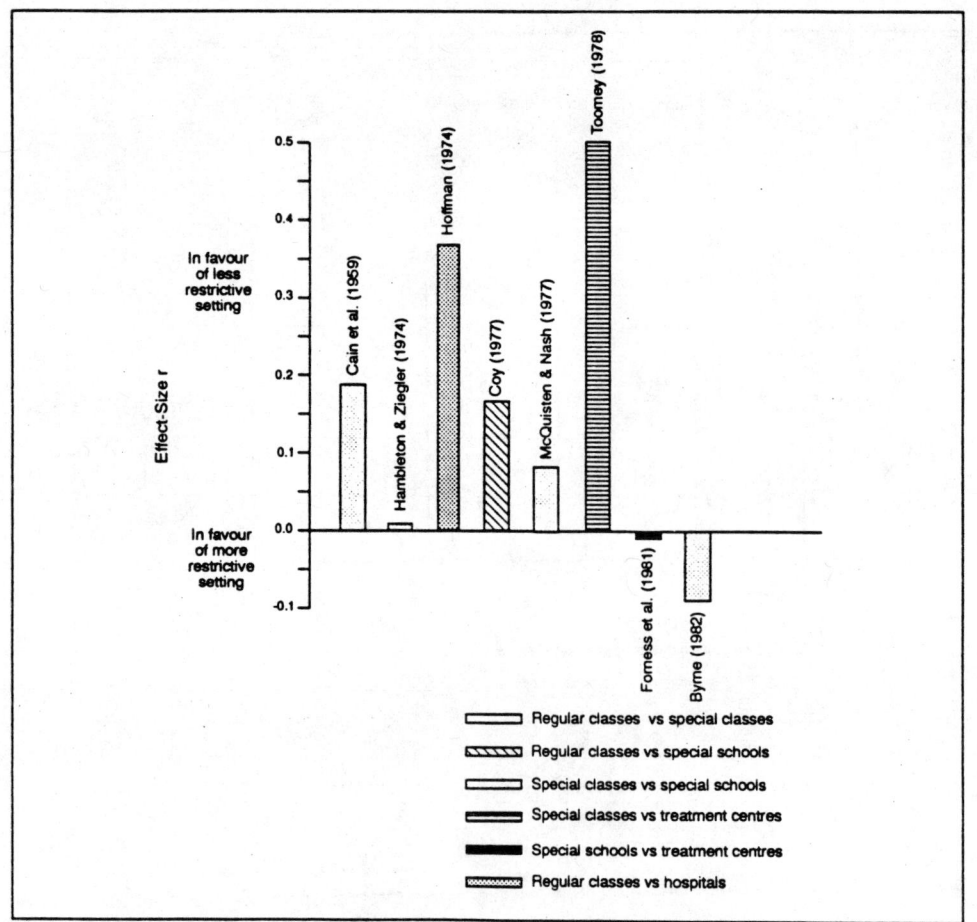

Figure 5.6 Effect Sizes for Adaptive/Social Behaviour Measures

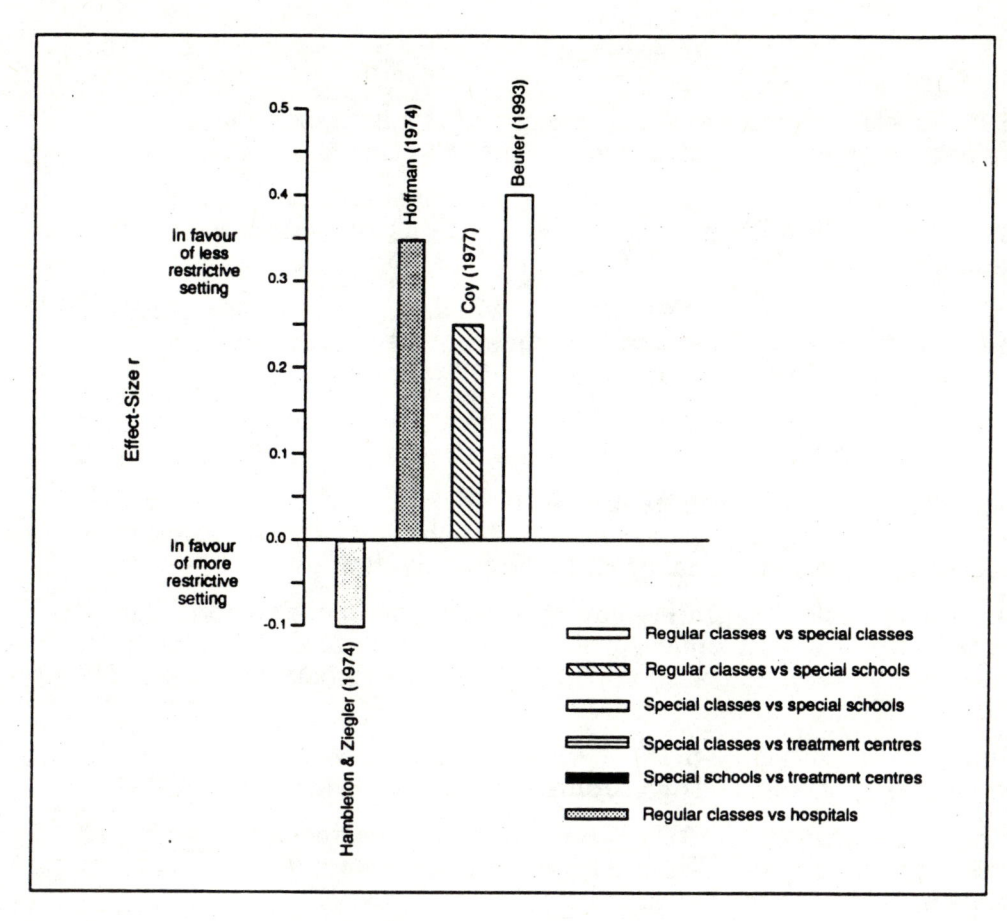

Figure 5.7 Effect Sizes for Motor Development Measures

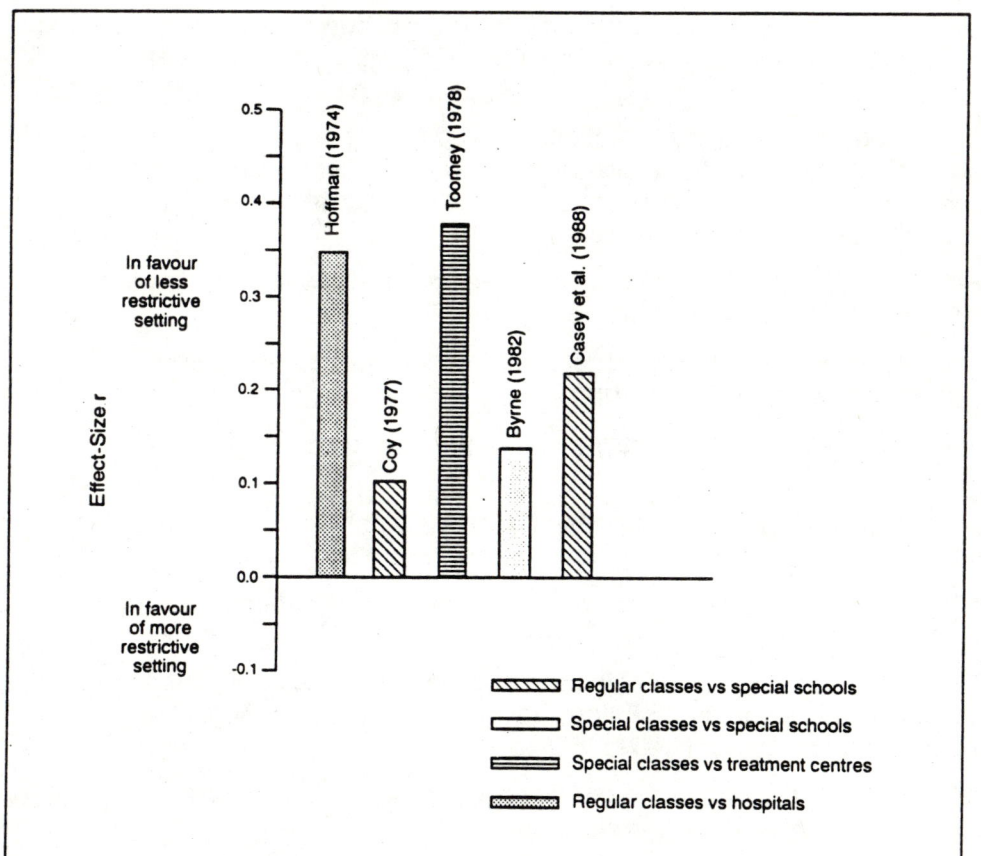

Figure 5.8 Effect Sizes for Intellectual Development Measures

85

References

Beuter, A.C. (1983). Effects of mainstreaming on motor performances of intellectually normal and trainable mentally retarded students. **American Corrective Therapy Journal, 37,** 48-52.

Byrne, B.M. (1982). **Semi-integration of mentally retarded children into the regular elementary school system.** Toronto: Ontario Ministry of Education.

Cain, L.F., Levine, S., Freeman, I., Elzey, F., Bake, L., & Moss, J. (1959). **Study of the effects of special day training classes for the severely mental retarded.** San Francisco, CA: San Francisco State College. (ERIC document ED 002-869).

Calberg, C. and Kavale, K. (1980). The efficacy of special versus regular class placement for exceptional children: A meta-analysis. **Journal of Special Education, 14,** 295-309.

Casey, W., Jones, D., Kugler, B., and Watkins, B. (1988). Integration of Down's syndrome children in the primary school: A longitudinal study of cognitive development and academic attainments. **British Journal of Educational Psychology, 58,** 279-286.

Coy, M.N. (1977). **The effects of integrating young severely handicapped children into regular preschool headstart and child development programs.** Sacramento, CA: California State Department of Education. (ERIC Document Reproduction Service No. ED 149 498).

Forness, S.R., Guthrie, D., and MacMillan, D.L. (1981). Classroom behaviour of mentally retarded children across different settings. **Journal of Special Education, 15,** 497-509.

Goldstein, H., Moss, J., and Jordan, J. (1966). **The efficacy of special class training on the development of mentally retarded children.** (Cooperative Research Project #619). Washington, DC: U.S. Office of Education.

Hambleton, D., and Ziegler, S. (1974). **The study of the integration of trainable retarded students into a regular elementary school setting.** Ontario, Canada: Ministry of Education.

Hoffman, D. (1975). A comparative study of institutionalized trainable mentally retarded children and implications for educational planning in the public schools of Minnesota (Doctoral dissertation, University of Minnesota, 1974). **Dissertation Abstracts International, 35,** 5169A.

Light, R. J., and Pillemer, D.B. (1984). **Summing up: the scene of reviewing research.** Cambridge, MA: Harvard University Press.

McQuisten, A., and Nash, C.B. (1977). Self-concepts of senior TMR students at a semi-integrated setting. **Mental Retardation, 15,** 16-18.

Rosenthal, R. (1984). **Meta-analytic procedures for social research.** Beverly Hills, CA: Sage.

Schneider, B. H. (1991) Reviewing previous research by meta-analysis. In B. Montgomory and Duck (Eds.), **Studying interpersonal interaction,** New-York: Guilford.

Slavin, R.E. (1987). Best evidence synthesis: Why less is more. **Educational Researcher, 16,** 5-11.

Toomey, J.F. (1978). A controlled experiment in the education of the severely subnormal. Paper presented at World Congress on Future Special Education, Sterling, Scotland. (ERIC Document Reproduction Service No. ED 157 300).

Witt, J.C. (1986). Teachers' resistance to the use of school-based interventions. **Journal of School Psychology, 24,** 37-44.

SECTION 6

PROVINCE-WIDE PERSPECTIVES ON PLACEMENT AND PROGRAMMING FOR DEVELOPMENTALLY CHALLENGED PUPILS

ABSTRACT

This section reviews the policies, placement practices, and plans for pupils identified as having moderate developmental challenges (referred to as trainable retarded at the time of the initial contract). The same methods of data collection as those described in Section 4 — focus groups, semi-structured interviews, and follow-up telephone interviews — were utilized to probe current policies and practices in selected school boards.

The general conclusion of the report suggested that there appear to be two competing visions of ideal services for Ontario's developmentally challenged pupils. One features optimal programming with the aim of maximizing the children's development; the other vision is one of community integration. The authors note that, in most circumstances, there is no inherent contradiction between these two visions.

Children with special needs in regular schools must be full members of that school community. The authors concluded that this is best achieved by intensive training for the regular staff and ongoing plans for using the total resources of the school in assisting youngsters with developmental challenges. It must be recognized that the education of developmentally challenged children is a costly enterprise, but one that is part of our responsibility as citizens.

Most of the focus groups expressed support for increased integration wherever possible. In addition, there is a need for clear curricula and meaningful evaluation of progress, despite the heterogeneity of this population and their developmental challenges. Programming would be facilitated by more appropriate assessment procedures for measuring both initial program/placement needs and attainment of objectives. The authors conclude by noting that a further research initiative by the Ministry in this area would contribute to maximizing these children's achievements and facilitate communication among major stakeholders. It would also maximize accountability in an era of rising costs and economic restraint.

Profound changes in the education of Ontario's developmentally challenged pupils have occurred within the memories of many teaching personnel currently working with them. Changes in Ontario law have brought these children within the public school system. Procedures for the identification, placement, and progress review have become essentially the same for developmentally challenged pupils and other youngsters with special learning needs. Finally, the needs of this group are now being met by both public and separate boards.* The legal status of special education programs in Ontario changed radically with the advent of mandated special education in 1985. In 1990, the Ministry of Education requested a review of policies, placement practices, and plans of selected school boards with regard to two groups of exceptional pupils. This section contains the review of policies, placement practices, and plans for one of these groups, namely, pupils identified as having moderate developmental challenges (referred to as trainable retarded at the time of the initial contract). We have already described a province-wide survey of the incidence of developmental challenges among pupils (Section 2) and a review of previous research on the comparative effectiveness of various placement options for this population (Section 5).

---

* Previous legislation mandated service to this population by public boards only.

As with the research study on behaviour-disordered pupils, multiple data collection methods were utilized to probe current policies and practices in the boards selected, the perceptions of major stakeholders about the adequacy of current programs and procedures, and their opinions about future needs. With the cooperation of contact persons in each school board, separate focus groups of administrators, parents, and teachers were organized in each of the 13 participating boards. Teacher and administration groups in each board reacted to standard hypothetical case descriptions, indicating how their board would handle the pupil in question. This method facilitated comparison of practices across boards, despite the fact that the pupils each designate as developmentally challenged might be quite dissimilar. All focus groups – parents, administrators, and teachers – participated in a semi-structured interview designed to elicit their perceptions. In the final stage of information gathering, telephone interviews were conducted between a senior administrator of each board and a consultant from the Faculty of Administration of the University of Ottawa. This last step permitted corroboration of the impressions left by the focus groups on an individual well versed in management but external to the special education field. It also provided an update on the views of the interviewees in light of changes in the economic climate surrounding special education services during the year that had elapsed between the beginning of the data collection to the finalization of this report.

Sampling Procedure

It was imperative that every attempt be made to determine an unbiased sample that would be reasonably representative of the province. Therefore, as in the case of behaviour-disordered pupils, it was decided to engage an independent consultant with appropriate expertise, Dr. Rama Nair of the Department of Epidemiology and Community Medicine, University of Ottawa, to generate the sample. Boards were selected randomly within each of five large regions (South, East, West, North, and Metropolitan Toronto) whose boundaries were delineated in the Ministry of Education directory. Census data were used to specify constraints on the selection. Accordingly, one separate and two public boards (one with large pupil enrolment, the other small) were selected within the Southern, Eastern, and Western regions. One public and one separate board were selected for both Metropolitan Toronto and the North. This resulted in the automatic selection of the Metropolitan Toronto School Board and the Metropolitan Toronto Separate School Board, the only boards in the Metro area serving this population at the time of the data collection. The automatic inclusion of these boards, while a violation of the random sampling, enabled the participation of the parents and teachers of the very large numbers of developmentally challenged children served by these boards. This procedure resulted in a somewhat higher representation of the Northern region and of predominantly French-speaking boards than their proportion of the provincial pupil enrolment. Focus groups were conducted in the French language in the two boards where it was the primary language of instruction. With the exception of the two boards in Metro, each initial selection was accompanied by two alternate boards in the same category. These were to be contacted in a pre-specified order if the first board declined to participate. It was necessary to contact the alternate boards in many of the regions.

Each board was permitted to decide which administrators would participate in the administrators' focus group. Local contact persons within each board helped derive a procedure for sampling potential participants for the focus groups of teachers and parents, taking into account geographical patterns within the catchment area as well as the board's organization of special services. Teacher focus groups consisted of teachers who had experience with developmentally challenged pupils in either special schools or integrated settings. In some large boards, the Research Department or Special Services Branch helped develop careful, elaborate sampling procedures for teacher and parent participants in focus groups. In most of the boards, sampling was not necessary, since all potential participants could be accommodated. In other boards, sampling procedures were more informal.

This procedure generated a sample that was reasonably representative of the province. However, as in all contemporary research with human subjects, there was no way of controlling for volunteer effect – the parent and teacher participants volunteered their time, and may have had some specific reason for doing so. While a wide range of opinions were presented at the focus groups, the sample may have presented opinions different from those of the parents, teachers and, indeed, school boards that elected not to participate. Table 6.1 summarizes the final sample of Ontario school boards that participated in this section of the project.

Teacher and administrator focus groups typically involved 10 to 15 participants. In contrast, parent groups were usually smaller, though invitations had been extended to many more parents. One board decided not to permit a parent group. In one other board, no parents arrived. However, parent participation was quite strong compared to the focus groups conducted by this research team in the same locations on different dates with parents of behaviour-disordered pupils.

The full text of all focus groups was transcribed. Research assistants who were not involved as interviewers extracted the major themes and categorized the responses for the synthesis reported below.

Hypothetical Case Studies

The writing team consisted of a school psychologist and a teacher/consultant. Both had extensive experience with developmentally challenged youngsters in school. They were instructed to write descriptions of youngsters who might be referred to IPRCs because of moderate developmental challenge. The case descriptions were to provide enough personal detail for them to be considered real. While features from the team members' professional experiences were allowed, these were to be composites of various children, with identifying features carefully disguised. The team members were instructed to develop case descriptions for which the optimal special education placement would be debatable. The team developed six case vignettes, of which two were selected as best representing a range of ages, genders, and problem behaviours. The following are excerpts from the case descriptions.

Table 6.1
Breakdown of School Boards in Ontario Focus Group Sample

	Separate	Public
North	1	1
South	1	2
Central	1	1
East	1	2
West	1	2

Tina, aged seven, is the youngest of the three children of a single working mother. Mom has been concerned about Tina's development since she was three years old, primarily because of slow language development and slow development of self-help skills. Tina now feeds herself with a spoon and sometimes uses a fork as well. Mom has taken great pains in toilet training, and now Tina does not have any accidents during the day, although at night she still wets occasionally. Her gross motor skills appear to be good. She can run and jump, and has started to ride a three-wheeler bicycle. Her expressive vocabulary is limited to 100 words, but she can understand 5-6 word directions. She recognizes 3-4 functional words (ladies, stop, danger) in context. She counts to 10, apparently by rote memory. The mother is very interested in, and insists on, sending Tina to an educational institution where she will have the opportunity to interact with children having normal learning capabilities. Tina's psychological assessment indicates moderate mental retardation.

Markus is an athletic fourteen-year-old with Down's syndrome. He still requires some prompting, but is basically capable of caring for himself (e.g., dresses himself after being told what to wear). He counts to 100 and can read simple sentences. He does well in environments with high structure, but becomes apathetic, disorganized, and occasionally silly in unstructured settings. The gap between his achievement and other children's appears to be widening as he grows older. Psychological assessment indicates that Markus is functioning in the moderate range of mental retardation, but his parents feel that he is higher functioning in many areas.

Method

Each case vignette was read to each focus group. After listening, the interviewer began with the following prompts. The participants were encouraged to elaborate on their responses. The interviewer queried responses with additional probes as necessary.

1. From the case description, where would this child most likely be placed within your school system?
2. In an ideal situation – where you could put together any program completely from scratch – what type of setting would you see as best for this child?
3. If money were no object, what setting would you see as best for this child?
4. If this child were older (younger), would your opinion as to the best placement be different?
5. If this child were lower functioning, would your opinion as to the best placement be different?
6. If this child presented more severe behaviour problems, would your opinion be different?

Results

Approximately three-fourths of the focus groups felt that Tina should and would be placed in a regular class with support. Many of these concluded that she was not likely to remain in the regular stream for much of her schooling, but would benefit from the peer contact in the first few years. Most stated that they would not be comfortable with Tina in a regular class if she were lower functioning or presented more severe behaviour problems. Several participants indicated that the parents' preference for the regular class setting was an important factor in their responses. A few of the focus groups, especially in the Northern region, felt that Tina should and would be placed in either a self-contained class or a special school. The pattern was reversed for Markus, with those advocating extensive integration in regular classes a clear minority. In explaining the differences in their responses, participants emphasized the age differences between Tina and Markus, and the curriculum demands of secondary schools. All groups said that their feelings about the optimal placement would be no different if additional money were available or if new programs could be started from scratch.

Conclusions

These results suggest that the majority of teachers and administrators are open to placing developmentally challenged pupils in the regular class setting under certain very specific circumstances. Differences in the child's age, behavioural profile, and functioning level seem to be important to the participants and influence their opinion regarding the child's suitability for regular class placement. Most of the participants assigned considerable importance to the parents' priorities and wishes, and expressed general acceptance of the need to respect the parents' aspirations. There were notable exceptions to these trends in some more remote areas where special schools for developmentally challenged are a well-established tradition.

Semi-Structured Focus Group Interviews

Method

Following the case vignettes, the interviewers asked a standard series of questions designed to elicit the participants' perceptions of the boards' policies and procedures regarding developmentally challenged pupils, the Appendix displays the standard interview prompts. Respondents were encouraged to introduce any additional issues they considered relevant to the major topics. The interviewers were instructed to probe as needed in order to understand the answers given to the pre-specified prompts and any additional issues that arose. A shorter series of prompts was used for the parent focus groups.

Results: Policies and Procedures for Identification and Assessment

Many participants, especially teachers in urban areas, felt that many of the children now being identified as developmentally challenged and placed in programs for the trainable are functioning at lower adaptive levels than in previous years. This is seen as relating to the trend towards de-institutionalization as well as changes in legislation over the past decade. In sharing these observations, the teachers did not seem to imply that these more handicapped children were inappropriately identified and placed, but that there was an increasing and unrecognized need for facilities, staff, and time in order to accommodate them.

Many of the teachers felt that they had much more to contribute to the assessment process than was being allowed. They felt that the day-to-day functioning of the youngsters in the classroom situation was the best single source of assessment information for this group of exceptional pupils. Nevertheless, some of the teacher participants insisted that the diagnosis of developmental handicaps should be conducted with increased care, using multiple sources of information and involving professionals of several disciplines. They indicated that such precision was essential since, once identified, the pupils' identification status is unlikely to change for years to come and may affect future expectations for the child. In addition to these concerns about the comprehensiveness of assessment procedures, the extensive waiting period before assessment troubled participants in some of the more remote communities.

A number of participants were critical of the tendency to apply the labels "trainable" or "developmentally challenged" to a broad range of child disabilities, resulting in a category that has little meaning by itself. However, there were no calls for abolishment of the category, nor any suggestions for alternatives. The intent of these comments was to advocate a more specific assessment process that would allow for more direct links between assessment and program planning. There was a common feeling that outside agencies completing assessments of these youngsters lacked essential information on their daily functioning. There were several calls for professionals conducting assessments to come into the school. There were also several reports of long waiting lists and lack of resources in French.

Results: Policies and Procedures Regarding Placement

Table 6.2 lists the major issues raised in the focus groups. There were enormous variations among the focus groups in satisfaction with the placement and review process. Many parents and teachers tended to feel disenfranchised, as if decisions had already been taken by the time they got to the IPRC. The attitude they perceived on the part of most of the people around the table was one of "What does a parent know?" or "What does a teacher know?" Many of the parents felt supported by local associations and advocacy groups. As well, some of the parents felt that they received very good support from principals and from teachers, especially kindergarten teachers, in understanding the IPRC process and placement options. Some of the focus groups observed that the well-informed, active parent of a developmentally challenged child would be successful in placing a child in the setting desired, but that parents with more limited resources might have difficulty in achieving similar results. However, some parents reported that even after they had officially "gotten their way", the schools often failed to deliver the promised partial integration – because of weather, staff absence, special programs, holidays, etc.

Teachers, parents, and administrators reported marked fluctuation among schools and teachers in their knowledgeability about developmental handicaps, and in their readiness or ability to receive integrated developmentally challenged pupils. The small number of developmentally challenged pupils results in further restrictions in placement options. For instance, pupils may remain with the same teacher for a major portion of their school careers. Some parents regarded this as highly undesirable. On the other hand, and especially in the larger boards, parents complained that the classes were being constantly reshuffled. Many teachers felt that self-contained classes for the developmentally challenged often enrol too wide an age range and too wide a range of functioning levels. Many parents, in particular, were highly attuned to the effects of classmates on their children's behaviour and learning, and resented the fact that peer influence was not considered in the placement and review process. Most but not all of the parents in larger communities favoured greater integration, though in one Northern community there was enormous support for a special school for the developmentally challenged. Some of the administrators considered integration a very costly enterprise, though many administrators insisted that cost was not a factor in their decision making. Others remarked that the transportation costs for self-contained programs were enormous, and that, aside from the costs, there were many problems with pupil behaviour en route to school, such as bullying. Several focus groups remarked on the very high cost of quality education for developmentally challenged individuals, and wondered whether taxpayers at large supported these expenditures.

A number of parents of children placed in classes for the moderately developmentally handicapped felt that their children might be able to manage in classes intended for children who are slightly less handicapped (opportunity classes). However, this was typically impossible, since the opportunity or GLD (EMR) classes were much larger than the classes for the developmentally handicapped (TMR) and had fewer teachers' aides and special services. As well, several teachers remarked that they were quite willing to have developmentally challenged pupils in their regular classes, but found that the supports offered in this situation were very inadequate. In several cases, a board would offer a wide range of costly services and assistance to children in self-contained settings, but would not provide regular services of even a teacher's aide at minimum wage for a youngster transferring from self-contained to regular settings. There were many similar reports of inadequate resources for integrated pupils, with some groups advocating more segregation strictly because of this. Many of the

Table 6.2
Major Themes Raised in the Focus Groups

Issues Raised — Behaviour Disordered	Administrators	Teachers	Parents
Annual Review of Pupil Progress	X	X	X
Articulation of Philosophy	X	X	X
Assessment/Diagnosis	X	X	X
Attitudes Towards Population	X	X	X
Availability of Services/ Programs	X	X	X
Board of Education – Roles and Responsibilities	X	X	X
Burnout		X	
Class Size	X		
Classroom Environment, Effects on Pupil Behaviour	X		X
Continuum of Services	X	X	X
Cost Factors	X	X	X
Counselling for Pupils		X	
Degree of Integration – Policy and Practice	X	X	X
Equipment Needs	X	X	X
Evaluation of Progress	X	X	X
Expectations for Students/Teachers	X	X	X
Expectations, Parents	X	X	X
Family as Cause of Behaviour Problem	X	X	
Immigrant/Refugee Students	X	X	
Increase in D.C. Students Over Time		X	
IPRC – Usefulness		X	X
IPRC – Time	X	X	
IPRC – Composition	X	X	X
Labeling	X		X
Local Conditions	X	X	
Mainstreaming	X	X	X

Issues Raised – Behaviour Disordered (cont'd)	Administrators	Teachers	Parents
Ministry of Education - Role	X	X	
Morale, Emotional Tone, Optimism	X	X	X
Parents – Involvement & Communication	X	X	X
Placement	X	X	X
Policy	X	X	X
Program Development	X	X	X
Program Evaluation			X
Pupil Employment, Work Experience	X	X	
Social Skills Training	X		X
Staffing, Child Care Workers	X		X
Staffing, Teachers			X
Staffing, Psychologists, Psychiatrists, Social Workers	X	X	X
Staffing, Teacher's Aides	X	X	X
Stigma, Ostracism, Social Rejection		X	X
Teachers, Preparation Time		X	
Teacher's Role	X	X	X
Training Administrators	X		
Training, In-Service	X	X	X
Training, Pre-Service	X	X	X
Transportation			X

teacher groups, including some teachers of self-contained programs, complained about obstacles in obtaining suitable equipment. Some of the administrators were well aware of this problem, and felt that it could be alleviated by clustering integrated students in selected schools where there could be a special effort at staff training as well as efficient deployment of resources.

Part-time integration was being widely practised, with some success. This seems to work best when there is good communication between the sending and receiving teachers, and when the receiving teacher accepts responsibility for participating in the child's program. In some of the larger boards, the teacher focus groups felt that integration was unsuitable for youngsters with major behavioural problems.

There were a few instances where self-contained classes within regular school buildings were administratively separate from the rest of the school. This is often the case in Metropolitan Toronto, though impending change in the structure of the school boards should alleviate this. Nevertheless, in some cases, the developmentally challenged youngsters and their teachers seem not to be fully welcomed in their schools. They might be served by special services personnel who do not serve other pupils with special needs and, in some cases, fall under the jurisdiction of a different superintendent. These unfavourable reports contrast with more positive experiences, including some reports of extensive contact between developmentally challenged pupils and other pupils in their schools.

Results: Review of Pupil Progress

Opinions were very mixed regarding the reviews of pupils' progress. Many of the teachers felt that the periodic review afforded an excellent opportunity for stock-taking. Many parents felt that the review was unlikely to result in any change in their children's placement or program. Indeed, some teachers and administrators mentioned that they were reluctant to try placement in a setting for higher-functioning children unless they felt it was very likely to succeed, for fear of difficulty reversing the decision should it later appear unwise. In any case, there was a general feeling that after a few years, parents become quite apathetic about the review process, and often fail to attend. On the other hand, many teachers felt that they were working under pressure to meet excessive expectations on the part of the parents. Parents, teachers, and administrators alike felt hamstrung by the lack of suitable yardsticks against which to measure the pupils' progress. This seemed to be less of a problem in larger boards, some of which had developed very detailed curricula for these programs.

Telephone Interview Regarding Policy Development

Method

The telephone interviews conducted by Dr. Jane Fulton, consultant from the Faculty of Administration, University of Ottawa, focused on the development of policy. Each participating school board was reached by telephone and asked for the superintendent responsible for special education or a substitute as necessary. Each participant was asked the following questions:

- Does your position make you knowledgeable about board policy and resource use for developmentally challenged children?
- Does your board offer segregated or integrated programs for this group? How has the board determined this policy?
- Do policies exist that describe criteria for student admission and staffing?
- Are policies in place that prescribe the allocation of resources to these programs?
- Do these policies drive resource use? Please describe how this works. Are trustees involved at this level?
- What effect will economic constraints have on these programs?

The interviews lasted an average of 30 minutes; some were longer. Detailed notes were made. A matrix was developed to give a cross-sectional depiction of the links between policy and the allocation of resources. Additional questions were asked as needed. It should be noted that these interviews focused on two groups of exceptional pupils simultaneously, developmentally challenged and behaviour disordered.

Results

The responses to the first few questions indicated that appropriate persons familiar with the boards' policies had been located. All subjects interviewed acknowledged that they were able to describe the policies and resource decisions affecting these programs. At the time of these telephone consultations, budgetary issues had become prominent in the administrators' thinking about the allocation of resources for the developmentally challenged. Most espoused a policy of integration as much as possible, but generally advocated a continuum of services, including self-contained classes where necessary. There seemed to be few clear guidelines for placement and programming. However, there was general acknowledgement that, in accordance with Ministry policy, parents' wishes regarding placement were given primary weight.

The respondents portrayed a situation that has prevailed over many years in which parents demand better programs for their developmentally challenged children. Special education advisory committees have served as a vehicle for these demands. The trustees and central board administration then finance the programming advocated. There was a general feeling that this sequence of events was about to reverse because of economic crisis, that "dollars will drive policy", and that integrated programs, which are seen as extremely costly, will be in great jeopardy.

General Conclusions

There appear to be two competing visions of ideal services for Ontario's developmentally challenged pupils. One, espoused by many teachers and administrators, as well as some parents, features optimal programming – life skills, speech pathology, adapted physical education, physiotherapy – with the aim of optimizing the children's development. The other vision is one of community integration, aimed at achieving peer acceptance, learning through observation, reduced stigma, and increased participation in community life. This second vision seems to be shared by most parents in urban areas and some school personnel. In most circumstances, there is no inherent contradiction between these visions. In theory, optimal programming can be delivered in any setting. In practice, however, this often does not occur. Most Ontario public school boards are accustomed to deploying special services and equipment to self-contained settings. At the moment, they seem quite prepared to honour parents' wishes, which often means placement in regular settings. But they have not always made the transition to different modes of service delivery. Current economic difficulties may affect the "start-up" expenditures needed to provide quality programming for integrated pupils in schools not already equipped for this. Pending accurate cost estimates, it might indeed be costly to provide specialized services and equipment in schools throughout a community even after a "start-up" period. In many of the participating boards the standing budget may basically provide for a self-contained setting, and then services for integrated pupils might be negotiated on an ad hoc basis, with excessive reliance on the limited resources of the regular receiving teacher. Providing special services to integrated pupils as an "add-on" may be ineffective but still be very costly. Better models for consultation, therapy, and practical assistance (e.g., supervised, trained teachers' aides) are sorely needed to increase the effectiveness of the integrated placements so many parents desire. Allowing parents the freedom to choose may not in itself expand the range of suitable placements.

Children with special needs in regular schools must be full members of that school community. This is best achieved by intensive training for the regular staff, and ongoing planning for using the total resources of the school in assisting youngsters with developmental challenges. The teacher of the developmentally challenged should be involved in extensive exchange with other teachers. It would also be beneficial if these teachers were rotated with special education teachers specializing in other populations, so that developmentally challenged children might receive more generic services, as advocated in most theoretical models of normalization.

It must be recognized that the education of developmentally challenged children is in any event a costly enterprise, but one that is part of our responsibility as citizens. There are perceptions of integrated services as highly costly, but clear and accurate data are hard to come by. Systematic cost estimates for special schools in the United States (see Lewis, Bruininks, and Thurlow, 1990) indicate marked fluctuations in the costs – fluctuations as large as 30 per cent of the budget – depending on the numbers of students congregated, transportation distances, and pupil-teacher ratio. Therefore, any generalization about cost in the absence of careful cost estimates may be premature. Nevertheless, our study of the perceptions of stakeholders strongly suggests that perceptions of cost figure prominently in the current thinking of many teachers and administrators.

Most of the focus groups expressed support for increased integration wherever possible. There was considerable feeling among school personnel, however, that regular class placement was only feasible for younger children not presenting severe behaviour problems. Support for special schools was limited to one Northern community, plus some large urban centres in the case of youngsters with severe behavioural difficulties. It should be remembered that our review of previous research documented no benefits of special schools. Since there was little resistance to the ideas of accepting parental wishes and integrating youngsters wherever possible, ideally it should be possible to avoid some of the adversarial situations that have occurred between parents and schools. We believe that this can be accomplished not by changing placement procedures or policies, but by organizing energy and resources to enhance the effectiveness and viability of the integrated placements many parents want, at the same time reducing the daily burdens faced by some regular receiving teachers we interviewed.

To a certain degree, improving the education of many developmentally challenged pupils in classes designated as serving pupils in the moderate range may depend on improvements in classes for youngsters with less severe problems. Some pupils might be able to learn better in classes where the peer group is slightly higher functioning if class sizes were not so large and support services were more often provided to these classes.

The heterogeneity of this population and their developmental challenges do not preclude the need for clear curricula and meaningful evaluation of progress. Programming would be facilitated with more appropriate assessment procedures for measuring both initial program/placement needs and attainment of objectives. These measures will surely incorporate more direct observation of pupils, as well as greater reliance on teachers and parents as sources of information. A research initiative by the Ministry in this area would contribute to maximizing these children's achievements and to communication among major stakeholders. It would also maximize accountability in an era of rising costs and economic constraint.

Reference

Lewis, D.R., Bruininks, R.H., and Thurlow, M.L. (1990). Cost analysis of special schools for students with mental retardation. **Journal of Special Education, 24** (1), 33-50.

APPENDIX
INSTRUMENTS USED IN THE SEMI-STRUCTURED
FOCUS GROUP INTERVIEWS

I. Questions Posed to Superintendents, Consultants, and Special Services Personnel

(after vignettes)

1. From the case description, where would this child most likely be placed within your school system?

2. What features of the case description led you to this conclusion?

3. In an ideal situation — in which you could put together any program completely from scratch — what type of setting would you see as best for this child?

4. If money were no object, what setting would you see as best for this child?

5. If this child were older (younger), would your opinion as to the best placement be different? Would your opinion be different if the child's behaviour were violent?

6. How does your board review the progress of behaviour-disordered and trainable retarded children?

7. How often are children transferred as result of these reviews? *or* (for developmentally challenged) How many youngsters have been transferred from programs for the trainable to other programs in the past two years?

8. Are there programs or services for these two populations that you feel should be established or increased?

9. Are there special programs for behaviour-disordered students who drop out or wish to leave school early?

10. Do you have estimates of the annual costs per pupil of the (various) programs for the behaviour disordered and developmentally challenged? Are costs for transportation included?

11. Do you have any statistics as to the graduation and drop-out rates for students identified as behaviour disordered?

12. Are there any training programs available for administrators or teachers regarding developmentally challenged or behaviour-disordered pupils?

13. What input do parents have to decision making?

14. What is your board's general philosophy regarding these two groups?

15. Are there any gaps in community or health services for these two groups?

16. Are there any changes planned in programs for these two groups?

17. Are there any specific local conditions that affect these issues? (e.g., language, culture, socioeconomic, advocacy groups, appeals).

II. Questions Posed to Teachers

(vignettes)

1. From the case description, where would this child most likely be placed within your school system?
2. What features of the case description led you to this conclusion?
3. In an ideal situation — in which you could put together any program completely from scratch — what type of setting would you see as best for this child?
4. If money were no object, what setting would you see as best for this child?
5. If this child were older (younger), would your opinion as to the best placement be different? Would your opinion be different if the child's behaviour were violent?

---

6. Is there something you would like to see your board doing for children like this that it is not doing now?
7. What supports do you as a teacher have in working with behaviour-disordered and/or developmentally challenged pupils?
8. What support and cooperation do you have from outside agencies or services?
9. Are there any gaps in services for these two groups in your opinion?
10. What approaches do you use in teaching behaviour disordered and/or developmentally challenged?
11. How do you feel about the fit between these children's functioning level and the school programs they are receiving?
12. Do you have adequate time to prepare programs for these children and work with them individually?
13. How do you feel about the placement process?
14. Are the physical facilities adequate for these students?
15. Have policies regarding these groups of pupils been discussed at local teachers' or Federation meetings?
16. How do you deal (would you deal) with children who are dangerous to others? Do (would) the school and board support you?
17. What is being done for behaviour-disordered pupils who drop out? Is more help needed?

III. Questions Posed to Parents

1. How well do you feel the board is providing for your children? Why?

2. Do you understand the board's policies and philosophies regarding children with special learning and behaviour problems?

3. Do the children's home behaviours differ from those in school? (If yes), to what do you attribute these differences?

4. How do you feel about the placement process?

5. Do you feel that the board's special programs are suitable and beneficial to your child?

6. Are there any special programs or services your child needs that are not available either in the school or in the community?

7. Has parent involvement been encouraged?

8. What information is shared and when does this take place?

9. Is there effective communication between home, school, and community?

Ministry of Education & Training
MET Library
13th Floor, Mowat Block, Queen's Park
Toronto   M7A 1L2